Innovatory Practice in Mainstream Schools for Special Educational Needs

Catherine Clark, Alan Dyson,
Alan Millward and David Skidmore

Department for Education
University of Newcastle-upon-Tyne

London: HMSO

Department for Education
Sanctuary Buildings
Great Smith Street
London SW1P 3BT

0171-925 5000

ISBN 0 11 270874 9

Contents

Executive summary

The research for this book was carried out in the period 1991 to 1993 and was supported by a grant from the Department for Education. It reports on findings from both primary and secondary schools, which were nominated by LEAs as having practice in respect of special needs which was regarded as innovative. No claims are made as to the extent to which every incidence of innovative practice is included, however, the authors are confident that they have identified the main trends in respect of the direction that practice and provision are taking in the area of special needs in mainstream schools.

A number of key issues are identified and discussed, and whilst the book does not provide a blueprint for schools to follow we are confident that the particular developments on which we report provide a framework in which special needs can be addressed. All of the developments that are identified were evolved before the 1993 Education Act and the Code of Practice were in place. Schools and their Special Needs Co-ordinators should be reassured to see the extent to which many of the requirements under this recent legislation were already being addressed in the schools identified in this research.

Although there are significant differences between primary and secondary schools at the level of the realisation of practice and provision the book argues that there is a broad similarity in the approaches that are emerging. At the heart of the approach is a commitment to locate provision for all pupils firmly in the mainstream class and to develop a repertoire of strategies which will ensure their access to an entitlement curriculum, thereby responding to a wide range of pupil diversity. Central to this endeavour are four key principles: the creative deployment of resources to support the learning of all pupils; the development of the school as an organisation able to respond to diversity; enhancement of the professional skills of all staff as the key agents of learning, and, providing a culture of collaborative support for staff and students by drawing on the widest possible resource base.

In the final two chapters these principles are elaborated and located within the context of the Code of Practice. The central message of this book is that schools which regard pupils with special needs as an opportunity to improve the provision for all their pupils now have the flexibility to develop their own innovative approaches.

1: Introduction

Special needs in the 1990s

The 1990s are already proving to be a time of considerable change in the educational world in general and in the field of special needs in particular. The implementation of the 1988 and 1993 Education Acts has set a context for the education system as a whole which has considerable implications for special needs provision in ordinary schools. Those schools are now faced by a situation which contains five major challenges:

- *They must ensure that all children have access to a common curriculum, which in the vast majority of cases will mean the National Curriculum.* As long ago as 1978, the Warnock Report stated that:

  'The purpose of education for all children is the same; the goals are the same. But the help that individual children need in progressing towards them will be different.' (Para. 1.4)

However, the 1988 Act takes this principle of entitlement much further. For the first time, the common curriculum to which all children are entitled is specified in detail and enshrined in law. Warnock's overarching goals become translated into subject areas, attainment targets and levels of attainment.

- *They must ensure that the particular needs of each individual child are met.* The Warnock Report and the 1981 Act gave protection to the small minority of children who warranted a statement of special educational needs. It sought to do this by, amongst other things, ensuring that those needs were effectively assessed so that appropriate education provision could be made. It was not felt necessary, however, to prescribe so closely the assessment and provision to be afforded to the 18% of children with special needs who were not the subject of statements. The 1993 Act and its accompanying Code of Practice (DFE, 1994a) on the other hand, can be seen as a restatement of the attention which schools must pay to the special needs of all pupils and not just those with statements. It does this in two main ways. Firstly, by obliging mainstream schools to demonstrate in their SEN policies how they make provision for *all* pupils with special needs, and secondly, by requiring all schools to have due regard to the Code of Practice in particular those aspects which require that provision and assessment for the 18% is as comprehensive and specified as that for the 2%. Schools and governors are thus given clear guidance as to their duties regarding all children with special educational needs.

- *They must assume increasing responsibility for the management of their own resources.* The 1988 Act introduced a system of local management of schools (LMS), enabling schools for the first time to take budgetary responsibility for their own affairs. This was part of a wider series of changes which had the effect of increasing the autonomy of schools and (in the case of maintained schools) of changing their relationship with the local education authority (LEA). In particular, resources and responsibility for special needs provision shifted somewhat away from the LEA and towards the individual school. These trends were extended by the 1993 Act and by the Code of Practice which set out in some detail the respective responsibilities of schools and LEAs. Given the increasing autonomy of schools, it is no accident that governing bodies are placed at the centre of these responsibilities. It is the governing body who must ensure that the detailed framework of the Code is implemented effectively and that the school deploys its resources to secure this end. The governing body must have due regard to the Code in approving the response that the school makes to special needs and must ensure that resources are deployed efficiently to achieve the necessary provision for pupils with special needs. They are likewise responsible for approving the special needs policy of the school which must be available to parents and must specify details regarding: provision; identification and assessment; staffing and training (Code of Practice, para. 2.10).

- *They must operate within a framework of increased public accountability.* In addition to the publicly available documents such as the SEN policy, there are now a series of other mechanisms through which schools are held publicly accountable for the quality of their work. The cycle of OFSTED inspections, the publication of examination results and other indicators of attainment, the availability of brochures and policy documents, and the monitoring of provision for all pupils with special educational needs and not just those with statements are all means whereby the wider community can gather information on the quality of its schools. The LEA will continue to hold a watching brief on the ways in which schools and governors are carrying out their responsibilities, and will continue to engage directly with the quality of that provision when pupils proceed from the school based stages of assessment to the more formalised statementing procedures. Similarly, the establishment of a system of independent tribunals to deal with appeals against the statementing procedures will further highlight the nature and quality of provision that schools are making. In these ways schools will be required to demonstrate that they are effectively implementing the requirements of the 1993 Act.

- *They must have particular regard to the wishes of parents.* As parents are increasingly able to exercise choice on the basis of increased information, schools are encouraged to be in tune with parental expectations and wishes. In making special needs provision, therefore, schools are faced with what might be regarded as a potential conflict. On the one hand, schools will have to satisfy parents of children with special needs that the needs of their children are being met, whilst on the other hand demonstrating to other parents that this concern with special needs does not detract from the education of other children in the school. In demonstrating that a concern with individual needs can actually enhance the quality of education in the school as a whole there is the opportunity to develop responses which reflect both individual site circumstances and the potential that exists at local or regional level for collaboration. Whether at an individual or local level, therefore, there is the potential for innovation to take place.

The situation which is created by these requirements is certainly one which schools experience as challenging. However, it is also one which offers schools the opportunity of responding creatively to the increasing autonomy which they can now exercise over the management and deployment of their resources. In terms of special needs in particular, schools no longer need to feel dependent on centrally-provided ideas and resources as to how provision should be made. As the implications of the legislation of recent years have become clear, there have emerged a growing number of examples of innovative and creative developments. In some cases, these have taken the form of the reconstruction of the relationship between LEAs and schools (Moore, 1993; Clark et al, 1990); in others the grouping of schools to form mutually supportive clusters (Lunt et al, 1994); and, in yet others, these developments have been evident at the level of the individual school (Dyson et al, 1994).

The Code of Practice, in restating and clarifying the requirements of the previous legislation will help schools and governors to review many of the existing systems and practices that are currently being used. For those schools that reviewed their special needs practice and provision in the wake of the 1988 Act the introduction of the Code of Practice will not be seen as a burden. In the course of that review some of these schools evolved creative and innovative responses which not only matched the new climate, but may also have seen them well-placed to meet the challenges and seize the opportunities of the 1993 Act and the Code of Practice. This book is concerned with describing and analysing the approaches taken by some of these schools. We do not claim that these schools offer a model to be imitated. However, we would suggest that teachers and governors have much to gain from reflecting carefully on the experiences of these schools.

Outline of the research

The research on which this book is based was concerned with identifying and analysing examples of creative and innovative approaches to special needs provision in ordinary schools. It was conducted in the period 1991 to 1993 at a time when schools were coming to terms with the implications of the 1988 Education Reform Act and when the issues which were to inform the 1993 Act were under active consideration.

All LEAs in England and Wales were invited to nominate schools which they regarded as having innovatory practice and provision in respect of special needs. We deliberately left the decision as to what constituted 'innovation' to the LEAs, since we did not wish, by being too prescriptive, to rule out forms of practice which might prove interesting. In analysing schools' responses, however, we were particularly looking for features which were both interestingly different from what was currently accepted as the norm and which seemed to be consistent with the demands of the new context.

The schools nominated by LEAs were contacted and asked to respond to a questionnaire about their work. Many of them also provided further information in the form of policy documents, handbooks, examples of teaching materials and so on. In addition to the request for LEA nominations, we took a series of steps to ensure that we were able to identify as many innovatory schools as possible:

all Grant-Maintained (GM) schools and City Technology Colleges (CTCs) were contacted directly and invited to contribute; articles in professional journals and presentations at conferences alerted schools to the project; and a range of contacts in higher education, professional associations and HMI were asked to nominate schools that we might contact.

These schools constituted a cross-section of all types of schools and their environments — from small first schools to large comprehensives; from schools with no statemented pupils to schools with on-site units; from rural schools in shire counties to inner-city schools located in areas of considerable deprivation. In all, some 109 primary and 88 secondary schools in the maintained sector responded, representing 57 LEAs. In addition, 3 CTCs, 12 GM secondary schools and 1 GM primary school responded.

On the basis of these responses, 8 primary and 12 secondary schools were selected for detailed case study. These schools were selected principally because they exhibited the major forms of innovation that were becoming apparent from the survey. We also, however, ensured that there was as much diversity as possible in terms of school type and environment. Members of the research team visited each of these schools, conducted interviews with the key personnel in the school's response to special needs — normally the head, the Special Needs Co-ordinator, class teachers and, wherever possible, the designated governor for special needs. We carried out observation of classroom practice where this seemed likely to clarify our understanding of the school's approach, and conducted detailed content analysis of a wide range of documentation supplied by the schools.

Our intention in carrying out both the survey and the case studies was not so much to evaluate the quality or outcomes of schools' work, but to understand as fully as possible the approaches they were taking to special needs and their reasons for developing this response. Having come to some understanding of these matters, we were careful to check our findings with the schools themselves and, where appropriate, with the nominating LEAs.

The research would not claim to have identified every single example of innovative practice in schools — indeed, we hope that readers will feel that their own schools' practice shares some of the innovatory features that we describe in the accounts which follow.

However, we would claim that we have identified all the major *forms* of innovation in special needs which were emerging immediately prior to the 1993 Act.

The structure of the book

We gave considerable thought to how best we might present the findings of our research in a form which would both do justice to the particular characteristics of the schools we studied and be of use to other schools in, perhaps, very different circumstances. In analysing the data, we were able to identify a number of themes which we believe characterised the features of innovatory practice in both primary and secondary schools and which, therefore, will be of interest to all schools. These themes were:

- *Teaching and learning: clarifying practice and embedding provision*

- *Resource management*

- *Managing change, managing roles*

- *Professional development*

- *Collaborative working*

At the same time, underlying these themes there are important differences between developments in primary schools and those in the secondary sector. These relate particularly to the tendency for most secondary schools to have in-house special needs teachers and departments whilst many primary schools rely largely on the work of class teachers. We have therefore opted to present findings in terms of the common themes, but to retain separate sections dealing with the primary and secondary phases. In the final chapters we draw together the themes and consider their implications for the current situation.

Governors and teachers may find it encouraging to note the ways in which schools were making creative responses to the situation as it obtained in 1991–93. Many of these responses are now even more relevant to the situation which has been created by the focus on special needs of the 1993 Act in general and the Code of Practice in particular. We hope, therefore, that governors and teachers will find in these accounts ideas and approaches which they can use to review practice and provision in their own schools.

2: The primary schools

Teaching and learning: clarifying and codifying practice and embedding provision

Innovatory practice in primary schools is characterised by:

a growing repertoire of articulated strategies for teaching and learning developed within and implemented by the school, enabling all pupils, including those with special needs, to learn effectively within the context of an entitlement curriculum.

Special need approaches in primary schools have traditionally relied upon the skills and expertise of the class teacher, whose job it has been to take responsibility for responding to the needs of all children in the class across the full curriculum. Where possible, the class teacher's work has been supported by the intervention of various LEA services including for example, peripatetic teachers with expertise in sensory impairment or remedial reading.

Despite the excellent work that has been carried out in many schools, there have been indications that this approach has not always worked to the full advantage of special needs pupils. Questions have been raised both about the rigour and appropriateness of some primary practice (Alexander, 1992) and about the effectiveness of links between classroom work managed by the class teacher and specialist interventions undertaken by the support service (HMI 1989). In the light of the Code of Practice, some primary schools will now also be considering whether they have in place the sorts of school and class-based programmes which will allow them to respond effectively to carefully-identified individual needs.

The schools which responded to our research project were keenly aware of the possible limitations of traditional primary approaches to special needs. Rather than simply relying upon the routine teaching strategies at the command of each individual teacher, schools were actively seeking to develop a range of specific strategies that could be used to meet particular children's special needs. They were not, by and large, looking to carry out far-reaching restructuring of their provision (in contrast to some of the secondary schools we shall report on later). Neither were they claiming to have discovered a single new solution to all special needs problems. Rather, they were bringing together a wide range of existing strategies and putting them into a manageable order so that they could identify what they were able to do for particular children in particular circumstances.

We can describe this process as one in which schools are attempting to clarify and codify teaching and learning practices. On the surface, this may not appear to be a particularly dramatic development but it is the careful articulation and effective dissemination of practice which is likely to see these schools well placed to meet requirements of the Code of Practice.

Schools were working along a number of dimensions to bring this about, and it may be useful to examine each of these in turn:

Assessment

Primary schools have always generated a good deal of information about the capabilities and attainments of pupils with special needs. This information has been derived from two major forms of assessment. On the one hand, *class teachers* working closely with their pupils have built up a wealth of knowledge about each individual. Unfortunately, this knowledge has often not been formalised or communicated in any but the most general terms. On the other hand, a good deal of assessment of pupils with special needs has been carried out by *specialists* (such as peripatetic teachers and educational psychologists) operating outside the classroom setting and outside the context of curriculum activities. Not surprisingly, it has been difficult in some cases to relate this assessment back to the teaching situation in order to develop individual classroom programmes.

The schools responding to the Project had not abandoned either of these approaches. However, they were attempting to develop for themselves a range of assessment strategies which were rigorous and explicit but which related closely to the curriculum and could therefore feed back into classroom practice. In some cases, this meant taking responsibility for the sort of diagnostic instruments formerly used by visiting specialists and combining these with teacher observation, sampling of pupils' work, records of achievement and profiles, and information supplied by parents. This information was not simply accumulated, but was collated by the Special Needs Co-ordinator — often in the form of centralised records or a register of 'at risk' pupils — and then disseminated to class teachers. This information then enabled class teacher and Special Needs Co-ordinator to collaborate in drawing up detailed individual teaching programmes for particular pupils.

In one school the co-ordinator had produced a detailed policy statement and written guidelines on the assessment process for pupils with special needs. This started from a statement of first principles — that:

'The assessment process is not simply concerned with establishing how retarded the child is in his/her attainments, nor with the nature of their difficulties, but with an understanding of the child as a person who has potentialities and strengths as well as difficulties . . . '

and that, therefore, assessment should take the form of an ongoing process which continually seeks to identify the possibilities for change. The policy then proceeds to set out a range of strategies which might be used these include:

● classroom observation of children, perhaps in collaboration with colleagues

● the use of appropriate tests 'as part of a comprehensive monitoring and screening procedure'

● the sampling of children's work

● the careful monitoring and recording of progress in curriculum activities undertaken by the class teacher but also involving pupils in monitoring their own performance

This information contributed to a three-stage assessment procedure (remarkably close to that within the Code of Practice). Assessment by the class teacher led on to collaboration between class teacher and Special Needs Co-ordinator and finally to the involvement of visiting specialists.

This school was not the only one to have undertaken similar developments in assessment procedures. A number of schools had organised assessment into a sequence of stages, so that they could differentiate appropriate levels of assessment, call on appropriate expertise at each level, and then match the level of intervention to the assessment. In each case, there was an emphasis on drawing upon the detailed knowledge of children that class teachers possess, but giving those teachers a structured framework within which to refine that knowledge, and ensuring that it could be supplemented by more specialist assessment as and when necessary.

It is perhaps worth underlining that the assessment process in schools was increasingly focused on children's performance within the mainstream curriculum. Although schools were continuing to make use of measures such as tests of attainment in literacy and numeracy, they were increasingly focusing on curriculum-based assessment processes. Drawing on the assessment expertise of their own staff not only enabled them to produce more detailed pictures of how individual children were performing; it also allowed them to feed that assessment back more directly into the teaching and learning process. Interestingly, some teachers commented that this shift in emphasis was increasing their understanding of the learning needs of all their pupils.

This close connection between assessment and teaching had led some schools to realise that the principles of assessment in special needs were not essentially different from those which apply to all pupils. Some teachers reported how they saw the monitoring of pupils with special needs as growing out of, and feeding back into the assessment and monitoring of the progress of all pupils through a common curriculum.

Developing teaching and learning practices

The close linking of assessment with teaching depends on the availability to teachers of a repertoire of strategies for intervening directly in children's learning. The schools responding to the project were not content to offer all children a standard classroom approach and then to call in outside experts for the children who experienced difficulties in learning. Rather, they saw children's difficulties as problems which it was the responsibility of the school to solve, and they sought to do this by having to hand specific strategies and responses which they could deploy.

One set of strategies rested on approaches more usually associated with special schools — the use of individualised teaching programmes, precision teaching, multisensory approaches to the teaching of spelling and reading, and so on. These initiatives were often collaborative ventures between mainstream and special needs teachers and can be seen as an attempt to import special education practice into the mainstream setting.

In other schools the emphasis was on differentiation within a common curriculum rather than on intervention outside it:

> One school had produced a lengthy document outlining a sophisticated approach which related differentiation to differences in interests and feelings, and which required the careful evaluation of classroom practice as well as the monitoring of children's achievements.

It was also interesting to see how information technology was being used to impact on children's learning and motivation:

> One school reported on how children from within the school had used the word processor to produce materials specifically for special needs work. Another school reported how it was using fax machines as part of a distance learning project to encourage pupils to develop their reading, writing and spelling skills. A further school made Dictaphones available to children with specific learning difficulties and encouraged parents to work through the recordings with their children at home.

The use of these strategies was by no means confined to the traditional 'remedial' areas of basic literacy. However, these schools also had in place explicit strategies for promoting children's reading. Characteristic of these approaches was the extent to which schools were trying to develop 'in-house' approaches to the teaching of reading rather than relying on external support. Some of these approaches were modifications of class teaching — the use of paired reading, the use of the DARTS (Lunzer and Gardiner, 1979) approach with young children, and reading 'blitzes' carried out across the whole school, for instance. Other approaches were based on individual interventions with particular pupils, such as the Reading Recovery Scheme (Clay, 1993).

The strategies reported by the schools had two important features in common;

● They were approaches that were *'owned'* **by the school**. In other words, they were devised by, or in collaboration with, the school's staff, and were implemented within the context of the school's routine provision. In this respect, they were different from traditional approaches which tended to be 'owned' by special needs teachers from outside the school.

● By the same token, many if not all were approaches which could *operate within the common curriculum*, not as alternatives to that curriculum but as a means of making it accessible to all pupils.

Furthermore, these approaches seemed to rest on the belief that the quality of learning is something which can and should be managed through the careful deployment of a range of explicit strategies. Such schools can be seen, therefore, as responding to some of the points raised by HMI (DES, 1989a) and Alexander (1992) in respect of a lack of differentiation, inappropriately narrow teaching strategies and topic work planned with insufficient rigour.

Managing behaviour

Although all schools, of course, have to manage the behaviour of their pupils, many of the responding schools felt it important to report specific strategies and interventions to the project. These included a variety of behaviour modification programmes, contracting with pupils and parents, and 'therapeutic' (Egan, 1973) approaches using music and drama (Mosley, 1991, 1988) as the basis of intervention. The significance of these initiatives would seem to lie less in the radically different nature of the techniques being used — most tended to be familiar forms of intervention — than in the acknowledgement by schools that pupil behaviour was indeed susceptible to planned intervention, and that such intervention should be seen as part of a broadly-conceived response to special needs.

In some schools this acknowledgement had led to the development of comprehensive policies and sets of guidance.

One urban school had produced a substantial handbook on all aspects of special needs, and devoted a significant part of this to the management of behaviour. This spelled out in some detail both the expectations of the school in terms of appropriate behaviours in school and the strategies that staff might use in order to secure that behaviour. Hence, it detailed routines, identified rewards and sanctions teachers might use, gave advice on individual counselling, set out the legal framework within which teachers must operate, and even went into detail on how to deal with children who are upset or who are having tantrums.

These sorts of developments echo the findings of Gilbourn et al (1993) about the ways in which secondary schools are responding to the recommendations of the Elton Report (DES, 1989b) by developing whole-school perspectives on discipline. Such developments will provide a sound framework within which these schools can respond to the recent set of government circulars on the management of pupil behaviour known collectively as *Pupils with Problems* (DFE, 1994b). Moreover, it is important to note how, in innovatory schools, the sort of whole-school approaches to the management of behaviour are closely paralleled by similar approaches to the whole range of special needs. Whereas in the past, both behaviour and learning difficulties have been seen as the responsibility first of class teachers and then of external agencies, these schools are coming to see both as demanding co-ordinated institutional responses, utilising the collective expertise of all staff.

Clarification and codification as innovation

It is perhaps worth underlining at this point the nature of innovation in teaching and learning in the primary schools reporting to this Project. It did not take the form of dramatic one-off changes. Much less did it take the form of radical departures from established practice or the discovery of markedly different ways of responding to special needs. Rather, it was characterised by the degree to which individual schools were seeking to bring together and make explicit their existing good practice. In doing so, however, they were able, often for the first time, to accept a high level of responsibility for managing their *own* responses to a wide range of special needs. It is in this acceptance of responsibility and this growth in autonomy and confidence that the innovation lies.

Managing resources

> ## Innovatory practice in primary schools is characterised by:
>
> an approach in which the school takes responsibility for managing its own resources flexibly in support of the learning of all pupils by: maximising resource availability; identifying and prioritising special needs resources, and establishing some interchangeability between those resources and mainstream resources.

Primary schools have traditionally had little or no flexibility over the management of their resources. Enhancement to capitation for special needs has usually come from directly provided LEA services over which the individual school has had little control. The introduction of LMS and the increasing devolution of resources from LEAs to schools has given all schools greater budgetary control. Schools responding to the Project had been able to take advantage of the opportunities which this presents. They were using the flexibility it had given them to seek ways of enhancing their resources and thereby impact on the response they can make to special needs.

Perhaps the simplest way of understanding how schools were setting about the task of resource management is to take the key innovative features of schools' responses point by point:

Increasing the volume of resources

The existence of a number of Government sponsored initiatives had led some schools to be pro-active in bidding for short-term funding.

This was not viewed as a way of sustaining permanent aspects of provision but as a means of pump-priming initiatives within schools which would have longer-term benefits.

In a number of inner city areas schools had benefited from a range of government initiatives which had targeted resources to particular priorities. A number of schools had focused on raising standards of literacy by using extra funding to promote and sustain home-school reading partnerships.

On occasions, initiatives which were not primarily targeted at special needs nonetheless had spin-off benefits for these pupils. Some schools reported how their successful bids for Section 11 funding were being used to promote staff development, increase parental involvement, and create a more favourable pupil-teacher ratio. Although these initiatives were directed at groups of pupils 'whose language and customs were different' (Local Government Act, 1966, Soc. 11), the schools reported that they had the effect of enhancing their ability to meet the needs of *all* children, and, in particular, those with special needs.

Clustering

Schools in some areas were 'clustering' as a means of creating economies of scale and the potential for enhancing resources in a particular school for a particular purpose. In so doing, they were anticipating recent government guidance (Code of Practice, para. 2.38) and form part of a much wider trend towards collaborative working (Lunt et al, 1994).

One cluster, which was the result of LEA policy, involved schools in bidding to the cluster for extra resources in respect of particular children or initiatives they wished to pursue. This system was to some extent capable of delivering resources quickly and flexibly to the point of need and it was reported that this had an impact on the level of demand for formal statementing procedures.

> Another cluster had originated largely from the initiative of a head teacher. It enabled participating schools to engage in joint ventures such as: the production of joint school literature; co-operative approaches to 'marketing' their schools in the local community; and the negotiation of the flexible use of LEA support services. In some schools, for instance, support teachers worked for blocks of one week rather than for part of every week thus making it possible to develop more flexible ways of working.

Integration as resource-enhancement

Many schools reported that they were involved in integration pro-grammes, and some were the location of bases or units for children with statements. Involvement in integration schemes created a flexibility of resourcing which had a significant impact on the school's ability to respond to a wide range of special needs.

> One school had been the location for a unit for children with moderate learning difficulties. As the process of integration had become more firmly established, so the barriers between unit and mainstream school had been broken down, with the result that the resources allocated to the unit were now more gener-ally available within the school. Hence, in-class support was now widely used throughout the school; the unit had been transformed into a resource base accessible to all children, including the more able; and the head of the unit had become part of the school's management team, contributing her expertise on a variety of issues.

This was not the only example of the resource benefits of integration. In a school with an EBD unit, for instance, the unit classroom was used by non-statemented children, and the teacher and classroom assistants attached to the unit worked in classrooms across the school. Interestingly, one effect had been that the school developed a sophisticated range of strategies for managing the behaviour of all its pupils.

Prioritising special needs

Schools reporting to the Project were characterised by an ability to identify resources dedicated to special needs as distinct from other resources. Being able to identify teachers, classroom assistants, co-ordinators, resource rooms or units as special needs facilities was a significant attribute of these schools, as was a prioritisation of special needs by heads and governors leading to a clear dedication of funds. This was reflected in the comments from a number of schools.

> One teacher in a grant-maintained primary school remarked, 'special needs is what this school is about', and the evidence for that was that the school had equipped a special needs resources base and employed a co-ordinator to manage it. In another school, there was a similar comment: 'Our teachers see special educational needs as being part of the fabric of our school', and the evidence again was the employment of a non-class-based co-ordinator and the dedication of significant amounts of the deputy head's time to special needs issues. In other schools, the prioritisation of special needs issues by the Governors was remarked upon, whilst elsewhere the relatively high level of resource and non-material support offered by the LEA to special needs was seen as important in enabling the school to develop its own approach.

Significantly, however, as remarks above indicate, the prioritisation of special needs was often equated not with the segregation of special needs as an area for separate provision and resourcing, but with placing special needs at the centre of the school's concerns. For the schools responding to this Project it was clear that they had gone beyond the rhetoric of, 'all our pupils have special needs', to a position where their concern was to meet the individual needs of all their pupils. In achieving this however they were able to demonstrate with increased efficiency what specifically they were able to do for those pupils who had special needs.

Staff deployment

In addition to their ability to identify dedicated resources schools reporting to the project characteristically displayed a creative approach to the deployment of special needs teachers across the school as a whole. Hence, although many schools continued to work with children in withdrawal situations, there was also a sense that withdrawal was a 'last resort'. Schools preferred instead to deploy their special needs teachers in ordinary classrooms, and many were actively developing a repertoire of flexible roles for such teachers which impacted on all children, not just those with special needs.

One school had produced a wide-ranging discussion document as the basis of a review of its special needs provision. Key themes throughout the document were the most effective use of limited support time, and the need to see the ordinary classroom and mainstream teacher as part of an overarching special needs strategy. Hence, support teaching was viewed not simply as the allocation of an extra teacher to work with special needs (in this case, statemented) children, but as a flexible resource, able to work with individuals or groups, or to free the class teacher to work more flexibly.

Managing material resources

Schools were displaying a similar flexibility in the way they managed material resources. Two trends were particularly noteworthy, and relate in part to the impact of integration units and bases. First, special needs resources were seen in some schools as whole-school rather than individual-teacher resources, and were accordingly housed centrally with easy access to pupils and teachers. Second, in some schools, the distinction between 'special needs' and 'mainstream' resources was blurred and special needs resources were made available to a wide range of pupils. One school was developing a central resource area for all pupils, for instance; another had a similar room equipped with photocopier, OHP and micro-computer; elsewhere an SLD school was making its Maths and English curricula available to children in mainstream schools.

Classroom assistants

The use of the classroom assistant as an unskilled 'extra pair of hands' was being questioned and schools were instead coming to look upon classroom assistants where they were directly managed by the school as a potentially valuable resource able to carry out a wider range of activities than had traditionally been the case. Hence, they were coming to be regarded as full teaching team members, and were involved in planning and review meetings. Where these assistants were employed as the result of a statement their main role remained that of supporting the pupil with special needs, but schools were increasingly looking at ways in which they could be used more flexibly often by working with a range of children rather than simply the individual to whom they were deployed by a statement. In some schools, they were offered training which equipped them with specialist skills more often associated with special needs professionals, thus enabling they to play a more extended role.

The examples quoted above would seem to indicate that schools are beginning to explore some of the opportunities which post-LMS funding arrangements give them. One final example may serve to highlight future directions.

One LEA had a long history of integration programmes between mainstream and special schools, which had developed into more formal partnerships between schools. One such partnership involved a special school for children with severe learning difficulties, which had outreach bases in nearby schools. Already, the special school was undertaking curriculum development and INSET activities for the mainstream schools, and the special school head was in the process of transforming one of her classrooms into a resource base for all local schools. She had plans to locate support teachers (from the LEA service which was in the process of being devolved to schools) in the base, and to offer a range of services to mainstream schools on a subscription basis.

Although this project was in its early stages, such collaboration between schools, particularly if it centres on the integration of statemented pupils and is, as in this instance, managed creatively, seems to offer mainstream schools a level and flexibility of resourcing which might not otherwise be available. As such, it may offer a way forward as LEAs increasingly devolve their special needs budgets to schools.

Resources: problems and issues

It is worth noting that even in these schools there were some expressions of concern over future levels of resourcing. As one governor said her concern was whether:

'we can, in the present circumstances, keep going what we've got.'

Another head commented:

'From our devolved LMS budget we have appointed additional classroom assistants to support [special needs] children, and also a 0.3 SEN teacher to give additional help with basic academic skills. How long the budget will enable us to do this remains to be seen.'

A response from a third school concluded:

'Generally speaking, there is a lot of good practice in SEN in this school, but since September '92 we have been severely under-staffed and SEN has been curtailed. [The LEA] is hoping to consolidate its SEN provision and will issue a consultation paper in the spring. Desperate days!'

It is worth noting that responding schools were not, by and large, arguing that substantial increases in resources were necessary to enable them to manage special needs provision, nor, in most cases, that their existing provision was under immediate threat. Their concern seemed to be that there was a delicate balance between demands and resources which could easily be upset by relatively minor shifts in funding. As one head put it:

'The existing integration model is very much dependent on the type of child in the school and the level of resources. If integration is to succeed, special consideration must be given to fine balance between the needs of the individual child and the school's ability to deploy existing resources. Our model is working well at present but given a change to any part of the "SEN equation" then the consequences of that change may well jeopardise the existing model.'

The implication would seem to be that schools can do much for themselves by seeking to maximise resources, by prioritising special needs, and by deploying their resources flexibly to meet children's special needs. However, they are crucially dependent on having a margin of flexibility in their resourcing out of which they can construct a special needs approach. Traditionally, that flexibility has been provided by the availability of LEA peripatetic teaching services. The downside of this, however, is that such services were never 'owned' by the schools and the approach may often have been the LEA's rather than the schools. As budgets are increasingly devolved to schools, therefore, it is not surprising that the element of ownership is increasing, while at the same time the level of anxiety is also rising as to whether the margin of flexibility will continue to be protected.

Managing change, managing roles

Innovatory practice in primary schools is characterised by:

a view of effective provision for pupil diversity as requiring change and development throughout the school; such a view operationalised through strategies for promoting change, managed by the headteacher but involving the Special Needs Coordinator in an extended role.

As we discussed in previous sections, the tendency in primary schools has been to regard special needs as something exclusively the province of the class teacher or a function of an externally-provided service. Either way, special needs has often been seen as having minimal implications for the overall management of the school. However, it will be evident from the developments we have described that the emerging approaches to special needs permeate many aspects of the life of the school. The developments in assessment, managing learning and managing behaviour, for instance, have implications both for how individual teachers work and for how that work is integrated into a coherent whole. Similarly, heads and governors are having to come to terms with managing resources for special needs as an integral part of managing the overall resourcing of the school.

It is not surprising, therefore, that we found a tendency in the schools in our survey for special needs to be a central issue in the management of the school as a whole. More than this, however, the process of management was increasingly interpreted not simply as the maintenance of the *status quo*, but as the continuing development and improvement of the quality of education offered by the school. Special needs was seen as central to this process, providing a key indicator as to the effectiveness of the school in delivering a full entitlement curriculum to all its pupils.

These developments were evident in the emergence of a number of strategies for change:

Monitoring and review

We have already seen how schools were developing sophisticated strategies for monitoring and assessing pupils. However, some schools were also extending this approach into the careful monitoring of the quality of their provision for these pupils. This then formed the basis for programmes of change and development.

Inevitably, the strategies used varied from school to school, but three examples may serve to illustrate the trend:

One school had produced a substantial handbook of guidelines for staff in respect of special needs, which not only offered advice on how children's attainments and needs might be assessed, together with suggestions for teaching strategies, but also provided a set of self-evaluation questions for teachers — with the implication that special needs might be met through changes in classroom practice rather than interventions with individuals.

Another school had decided to reconsider the role played by its unit for children with moderate learning difficulties and to move to a more fully integrated approach. It tackled this not by producing a detailed development plan, but by setting a series of broad targets and linking these to review questions ('What use is made of reports on children?' 'How is the unit expertise used throughout the school?') and issues for discussion ('How do we use the support teacher, ancillaries and parents? Do we extend teacher provision or do we develop a team of ancillaries led by a teacher/co-ordinator?')

In a third school there was an ongoing programme of classroom observation in which all staff were, as far possible, participating. This programme functioned not only as a form of professional development, but also highlighted issues for consideration at a whole-school level. The head expressed the view, for instance, that the school had been able to anticipate much of the critique of 'received' primary practice in the Alexander Report (1992) as a result of looking carefully at its own practice.

Formalisation and planning

All schools are engaged in processes of planning to implement the National Curriculum. In the schools which reported to us, however, the planning process was being used not simply to manage the logistics of the curriculum, but to ensure that the meeting of individual needs and the delivery of an entitlement curriculum to all were forming a coherent whole. In doing this, these schools were breaking out of the traditional mould of regarding special needs as part of the private domain of the class teacher or support service teacher, and were further involved in the clarification and codification of practice which we described above.

This trend can be illustrated by reference to a large (460+ on roll) junior school located close to a military base with its inevitably somewhat transient population:

In addition to this transient population, the school was the site of a 10-place unit for children with moderate learning difficulties, though in recent years it had progressively broken down the barriers between the unit and the mainstream classes, The head teacher saw special needs as a priority in the school, and the head of unit was a member of the school's senior management team so that she could be involved in strategic planning. Indeed, a high level of planning was seen as the most effective way to meet the diverse demands which the school faced. This was evident in two main respects. First, there was a

27

highly structured approach to special needs provision — a staged assessment procedure, formalised support procedures, regular meetings and exchanges of information between specialist staff, classroom assistants and class teachers.

Second, this structured special needs approach was part of an overall approach to the development of practice and provision within the school. Teachers were not left to work in isolation but were involved both in year-based curriculum planning groups and in issue-based working parties. These groups were co-ordinated in two ways. The year-based planning groups met regularly with the senior management team of the school to consider implications arising from their work — including implications for special needs provision. The issue-based groups had a life-span of a year, at the end of which they were required to make a presentation to the whole staff, including support staff.

As the head pointed out, this was a school in which teachers had historically 'done their own thing'. The development of a high level of planning was, in effect, the only way that the school could ensure both the effective implementation of the National Curriculum and the progressive functional integration of the pupils from the special unit.

It is typical of the schools responding to this Project that planning was not seen in this school as a once-for-all process. The development of increasingly sophisticated responses to special needs was seen in this school as an ongoing process; it was about *continuous but orderly change* rather than the maintenance of the status quo. This in turn had implications for the nature and purpose of policy formulation in this and other responding schools.

On a number of occasions, we have referred to schools' policy documents and booklets of guidance for staff — and this is no accident. Schools responding to the project tended not simply to be able to produce impressive levels of policy documentation, but to have produced documents which actively guided practice. The special needs and behaviour policies we have referred to were not simply brief statements of general principle nor schematic outlines of current procedures. On the contrary, they were detailed accounts of the school's current understanding of 'good practice'.

These documents served a number of purposes. First, they acted as reference points for both new and existing staff, giving them help and advice on how to respond to particular special needs in the classroom. They thus acted as a stimulus to the development of individual teachers' practice. Second, they established a common approach across the school, thus seeking to develop a level of consensus and coherence across the staff as a whole. Third, by making practice public, they made it possible for teachers to review and develop the school's notion of good practice. In these ways, school policies formalised practice, promoted planning and acted as catalysts to change and development.

External initiatives

The history of external catalysis of school development is a somewhat mixed one, but there was evidence from responding schools that such initiatives could offer schools a framework within which to manage their own change processes:

In the cluster system referred to earlier, the large scale devolution of resourcing and responsibilities appeared to be acting as a catalyst for change. A headteacher, who acted as a 'family group's' Special Needs Co-ordinator spoke of how the system had encouraged an 'extended view of professional life' within the staff of particular schools, how it enabled schools to share practice and concerns, and to think carefully about their use of resources.

These views were endorsed by an LEA which had adopted auditing systems to allocate special needs resources. What seemed to be crucial here was that although the initiative originated externally, there was ample scope for the school to take it forward, interpret it in its own way, and establish 'ownership' over the resulting practice and provision. The family group system, for instance, was described as 'giving responsibility with resources'. The responsibility element seems to have allowed schools to see this externally-imposed initiative not as a constraint, but as an opportunity for them to meet new challenges in innovative ways.

The co-ordinator as change agent

Traditionally, as HMI point out (DES, 1989a) the role of the Special Needs Co-ordinator in primary schools has been somewhat ambiguous, many co-ordinators have in fact been either full-time class teachers or heads or deputies for whom this was an additional responsibility. In either case, they have had the title of co-ordinator but have often had very little time in which to be proactive in the role. There have been other problems. Not all co-ordinators have felt confident that they have sufficient expertise to undertake the role effectively, and this has compounded the difficulties they have faced in intervening in the work of their colleagues (Dyson, 1991, 1990). Moreover, most direct individual work with children with special needs has not been undertaken by the co-ordinator at all, but by outside agencies and support services.

In the schools responding to us, by contrast, co-ordinators were beginning to define for themselves a very different sort of role. Increasingly that role is one which is involved in developing strategy at whole school level and also in developing the classroom practice of every member of the school staff. Schools reported that *the co-ordinator was becoming a manager of organisational change and development*. This view of the role led such co-ordinators to be proactive in introducing a range of initiatives in schools.

The extended nature of the role of the co-ordinator can be seen in one example which is not altogether untypical:

> The Special Needs Co-ordinator in a multi-cultural school in an outer London Borough is non-class based, but is fully timetabled so that all staff have special needs support in a given year. Although not a member of the Senior Management Team, she works closely with the deputy head who takes responsibility for children with behaviour difficulties. Moreover, she plays a full part in whole-school development, attending a wide range of planning meetings and not just those which have a special needs focus. Rather than simply working with children directly, her role is to work closely with staff in order to help them to identify and make provision for special needs. She is therefore active in helping colleagues with the differentiation of the curriculum and supports them in the development of individual programmes for particular children. In effect, therefore, she has a professional development role, and this is particu-

larly evident in her contribution to the school's Teacher Support Team (Norwich and Daniels, 1992) which provides a forum within which teachers can exchange ideas on special needs and share problems, thus overcoming the feeling of working in isolation.

It was apparent that 'extended' co-ordinators, operating in this way as managers of change and development were able to sustain their role because of three key qualities:

- They had a high level of credibility amongst their colleagues, which was in large measure earned because of their ability to support both pupils and staff effectively. Many emphasised the importance of collaborating closely with colleagues on practical teaching problems. As one put it, 'I try to work hand in hand with the teachers.'

- They had a level of expertise in special needs teaching which supplemented the class-teaching expertise available to their colleagues. This was particularly the case where the co-ordinator was managing a facility for statemented pupils — though not every effective co-ordinator was a special needs 'specialist' in this sense.

- They tended to have a broad perspective on their work, sometimes stemming from experience outside traditional class teaching or mainstream special needs work. One co-ordinator, for instance, had been an LEA advisory teacher; another had trained as an educational psychologist.

To carry out this extended role, co-ordinators in the case study schools were given some non-contact time, some of which was to support pupils and some to work with colleagues in their classrooms. More often, however, these co-ordinators saw themselves filling a more developmental and consultative role which led to the breaking down of some of the traditional barriers between classrooms and demanded a new set of skills. As one co-ordinator put it:

'I feel that I do not want to be cast in the role of expert. I prefer to be seen as a member of the team. I try to provide the opportunity for staff to get things off their chest and, in doing so, become involved in solving the problem with me. Often the best thing I can do is find time to talk things through with people.'

Head teacher as change agent

It is arguable that, in the past, headteachers could discharge their responsibility in respect of special needs by securing the services of a specialist teacher or — more probably — of the LEA's support service. However, a notion of special needs provision which requires whole-school planning and development also requires the full involvement of the headteacher.

It was notable in responding schools that headteachers were instrumental in all the sorts of development we have reported above. The management approaches of these headteachers appeared to share three characteristics:

- Their management of the school in general and of special needs in particular was underpinned by an explicit commitment to clearly articulated principles; notions of equal opportunities, human rights and curriculum entitlement were common in their responses.

- They were able to see the inter relatedness of 'special needs' and 'mainstream' issues. As one head put it, 'Our work with SEN children is so well integrated and underpins so much of the work of the school, it is difficult to separate mainstream and special provision. We try to provide a continuum of provision for every child'. As a result, they were willing to devote resources to special needs, to integrate special needs provision into the mainstream, to involve the co-ordinator at management level, and to promote the use of 'special needs' strategies throughout the school.

- Despite their close involvement in special needs issues, they were willing to appoint and empower well-qualified and forceful Special Needs Co-ordinators who then operated with a high level of autonomy. Far from being threatened by the prospect of such 'loose cannons', they appeared to see them as major instruments of change.

The result of this approach from headteachers was that, in many cases, they were able to create a framework within which special needs became a genuinely whole-school issue, special needs teachers could operate across the school as a whole, and change and development became a part of the school's culture.

Professional development

Innovatory practice in primary schools is characterised by:

a view of the professional expertise of all staff as an essential resource in the school's response to pupil diversity, to be enhanced through school-centred professional development strategies.

In many schools responding to the Project an interesting model of professional development was emerging. It appeared to be under-pinned by two assumptions: that high-quality special needs provision necessitated the professional development of *all* staff, including classroom assistants and, in some cases, parents as partners in the teaching process; and that such professional development should be firmly rooted in its context — that is, that it should relate to particular problems facing particular teachers, and should, to a large extent, seek to enhance the skills those teachers already possessed, rather than initiating them into a new expertise.

These assumptions manifested themselves in a number of forms of professional development activity:

- *Formal INSET activities* constituted a significant part of schools' professional development programmes. Teachers continued to attend courses and institutions of higher education or local authority centres, and specialist trainers were imported into schools to run training sessions. However, much formal INSET was school-centred in being led by the school's own staff (often the co-ordinator), and responding to staff's perceived and expressed needs. In some schools, the co-ordinator had the organisation of school-based INSET as part of their formal job description.

- Some professional development was less concerned with formal 'delivery' sessions than with *research and inquiry* processes. A number of activities that we have reported on can be seen in this light. The careful monitoring of pupil progress, the monitoring and review of curriculum, the collaboration between Special Needs Co-ordinators and class teachers and the joint approaches to planning and policy-formulation can all be seen as means whereby schools are developing a clearer understanding of their own practice and of its effectiveness. This approach does not restrict itself to equipping teachers with new skills. Rather, it has a view of practising teachers as active problem-solvers capable, with appropriate support, of developing both their own practice and the overall response of the school. As one head teacher said, 'we are sitting on a wealth of knowledge and understanding'.

- In some schools, Special Needs Co-ordinators saw their presence in colleagues' classrooms as serving more than the obvious purpose of supporting particular pupils. It provided them with an opportunity to *model* particular techniques and strategies in a non-threatening and supportive way.

Two further aspects of responding schools' approaches to professional development were apparent, particularly in the case study schools. First, the Special Needs Co-ordinators who played such a key role in the development of colleagues, were themselves 'self-developing professionals'. They had strategies — attending courses, linking themselves into LEA and other networks and working closely with other professionals — to maintain the momentum of their own development.

Second, by pursuing strategies of professional development that were school-centred, schools were effectively breaking away from what might be seen as their traditional dependence on external expertise. Implicit in their approach was the assumption that human resource development is a key part of schools' responses to special needs, and that such development can and should be internally-driven. There are, of course, dangers of parochialism and of the recycling of bad practice in this approach. However, the principled stances of head teachers, the broad perspective of co-ordinators, the willingness to respond to external initiatives and the participation of some schools in clustering arrangements seemed to offer safeguards which turned school-centredness into a strength rather than a weakness.

Collaborative working

Innovatory practice in primary schools is characterised by:

the establishment of collaborative working arrangements both within and beyond the school in order that schools and teachers might be effective in making provision for all their pupils, thus becoming less reliant on external interventions.

Much of what has been reported in preceding sections implies a high level of collaboration between staff, schools, LEAs and other partners in the educational process. Some specific features of this trend towards collaborative working deserve to be highlighted.

Internal collaboration

We have already seen the extent to which schools responding to the Project had systems and structures which encouraged staff to work together. These structures took a variety of forms, ranging from simple collaborations between small groups of staff sharing responsibility for classes and key stage groups through to the sort of elaborate decision-making, planning and monitoring mechanisms referred to in the section on 'Formalisation and Planning'.

The key issue is less the particular form of collaboration than a recognition by individual teachers and the school as a whole that the management of effective responses to a range of individual differences was not possible if teachers worked in isolation. Only by sharing ideas, resources and plans could a coherent approach to individual entitlement be formulated. In many respects, of course, this marks a significant departure from the traditional model of primary school organisation. It also underlines the key role played by the headteacher as overall manager of this collaborative response and by the Special Needs Co-ordinator as the catalyst and facilitator of this process.

External collaboration

In a similar vein it is possible to identify some specific developments which relate to a notion of external collaboration. Two such partnerships are of particular interest:

Parents and the community

The notion of 'parents as partners' has long been a familiar theme in primary and special needs education (Wolfendale, 1989). It is not surprising, therefore, that many of the responding schools chose to report initiatives in this area. Some of these schools were distinctive in the way they set about increasing parental involvement. Rather than waiting for parents to come forward, they were highly proactive both in seeking parents out and in consciously developing the ability of parents to be involved constructively in their children's education.

> One school was located in an area with significant social and economic problems. Far from regarding this as a difficulty in developing partnership with parents, the school viewed it as all the more reason to become involved with the community. It made full use of whatever external funding it could secure in order to enable teachers to take a proactive role in the community, working closely with parents to explain the work of the school and secure their support over issues such as attendance. They also offered support to parents — particularly parents of children with special needs — in finding their way through the education system, arguing that
>
> 'People in this area do not know how to fight for themselves and we help them. They struggle with documents like statements of special needs as well as with the English education system, so close liaison with parents is important.'
>
> As the headteacher commented:
>
> 'We must not assume that our parents are not concerned about their children; we must find ways of showing that we value what they do and encourage them to participate actively in the life of the school.'

This school and other schools responding to the Project, had a view of their relationship with parents and the community which amounted to more than a conventional expectation that parents would automatically support the school. They saw this support as something that had to be worked for by the school becoming proactive in the community, serving as a resource to its parents and going out of its way to share skills and expectations with the parent body. The vehicles for this approach — shared reading schemes, parents' workshops, home visits and the like — were not in themselves remarkable. They were, however, able to be used in a sustained and coherent manner because of the schools' management of resourcing. One major resource was the commitment of the staff. Over and above this, however, was the search for means to supplement the schools' existing resources externally. As we have noted in the section on resources above, these schools had developed particular skills in bidding for funds from government-sponsored initiatives and were then prepared to target these funds carefully towards projects which would have long-term benefits in respect of parental partnership

LEA services and other schools

A crucial shift in relationship between the school and the LEA was reported to the Project. There has been a tendency in the past to conceptualise the support services provided by the LEA in respect of special needs as being targeted at individual children. As a result, the pattern of such provision has sometimes times been decided on the basis of a decontextualised assessment of individual need, with the consequent danger of operating in isolation from the policy and working practices of the schools in which the service was delivered.

There was evidence however, of the emergence of a more balanced partnership between school and LEA services. The most notable feature of this partnership was the extent to which both sides were working towards models of service delivery which were consistent with *school* policy and practice. Rather than the LEA seeking to direct centrally the deployment of services to meet its own priorities, there was an increase in processes of negotiation which took account of the sorts of approaches the schools were developing and the ways that LEA services might support those developments. Many schools, for instance, spoke about their increasing ability to make best use of support and psychological services. This was a particular feature of schools which were involved in clustering arrangements:

In two clusters, negotiations had taken place with the LEA support service for some form of provision other than the allocation of fixed hours to particular children. In another cluster the educational psychologist spoke of the change in her role which the cluster arrangement had brought about. Instead of being locked into statutory assessments of individual children, she was able to operate as cluster facilitator and consultant, helping schools to share ideas and engage in joint problem-solving, and thus fulfilling a more developmental rather than 'fire-fighting' role.

Two factors seem to account for this development. The first is that, as we have noted, schools were able to make their special needs practice more explicit, and were thus able to articulate for external agencies precisely what the pattern of provision was to which those agencies were expected to contribute. Second, the emergence of the Special Needs Co-ordinator in an extended role meant that agencies had not only a contact point but also someone who could work closely with them in building a genuine partnership. As a result, the collaborative working arrangements and formation of teams within schools was extended to include and involve LEA support teachers, educational psychologists and others.

Summary

For the primary schools in this survey there appears to be a conscious attempt to move away from a position where special needs is an issue which can be left to individual class teachers working in isolation, or handed over to external agencies. Instead, they are accepting a high level of responsibility for meeting the special needs of their own pupil populations. In order to do this, they are developing a repertoire of explicit responses to special needs which are available to all teachers and are co-ordinated into a coherent approach across the school as a whole.

This process is neither dramatic nor radical, but rather results from a continuous process of clarification and codification, formalisation and planning. It demands a high level of collaboration both within the school and between the school and various parts of its environment. It also requires the school to manage its resources flexibly and creatively so as to sustain its special needs approach. In this context, the skills of the staff constitute a major resource and professional development a key strategy. Above all, these developments cast the headteacher and the Special Needs Co-ordinator as key change agents within the school, and require the latter in particular to play a complex role extending well beyond the boundaries of the traditional special needs teacher.

3: The secondary schools

Embedding provision for pupil diversity

Innovatory practice in secondary schools is characterised by:

strategies for embedding provision for the full range of pupil diversity within ordinary classrooms and in the context of an entitlement curriculum, underpinned by notions of individual differences and supporting the learning of all pupils.

We have characterised traditional primary approaches to special needs as dependent upon a combination of the skills of class teachers working in isolation and of external agencies such as peripatetic services. The situation in secondary schools has been somewhat different. We would suggest that these schools have in most cases been large enough to sustain their own in-house special needs provision. Over the years, this provision has had many forms: special classes, remedial departments, withdrawal systems and so on. A common feature of all these forms has been that, although they have been located physically within the school, they have to a greater or lesser extent taught pupils with special needs in isolation both from the mainstream classroom and the mainstream curriculum.

During the 1980s, a significant attempt to address this issue was made under the aegis of the 'whole school approach' (Dessent, 1987). This sought to redefine special needs as an issue which concerned the school as a whole, and to involve all teachers in making provision for pupils with special needs so that those pupils could participate as fully as possible in a 'comprehensive curriculum'. Since the 1988 Act, the introduction of a National Curriculum as an entitlement for all pupils has once again highlighted this issue.

Unfortunately, it is far from certain that the whole school approach as commonly practised has achieved the full integration of pupils with special needs in the mainstream curriculum. Considerable doubts have been expressed about some of the main elements of the approach such as support teaching (Hart, 1986), the special needs co-ordinator role (Bines, 1986; Dyson, 1990) and, latterly, differentiation (Peter, 1992). The argument has been put that these have simply been 'bolted onto' forms of classroom practice and school organisation which have not themselves been sufficiently reconstructed to take account of the needs of all pupils. Certainly the findings of HMI (DES 1989a, 1990) suggest that the whole school approach has not been a universal panacea.

The issue for secondary schools, therefore, is not so much one of making their special needs practice and provision more explicit. In most schools, special needs teachers and co-ordinators have developed a range of specific skills and strategies for responding to pupils' difficulties. The problem is that those skills and strategies remain separate from routine practice in the school as a whole. The issue for secondary schools, therefore, is one of how to *embed* special needs practice and provision in every mainstream classroom. If secondary schools are to deliver a broad and balanced curriculum as an entitlement to pupils with special needs, then *all* teachers have to be capable of responding to those needs, and *every* classroom has to become a learning environment in which pupils can flourish.

Much of what the innovatory schools responding to this Project reported can be interpreted as an attempt to develop 'embedded' special needs provision in this sense. This is true in particular of certain features of their work:

Developing teaching and learning practices

Responding schools continued to use special needs teachers in direct interventions with particular pupils and asked those teachers to deploy 'specialist' skills that were clearly not expected of their mainstream colleagues. However, this deployment of specialist teaching was increasingly being set alongside conscious and coherent strategies for developing teaching and learning practices across the curriculum, so that the learning experiences routinely available in mainstream classrooms might be appropriate to a more diverse range of pupils. Hence, schools reported their involvement in flexible learning initiatives (Eraut et al, 1991), differentiation projects (Stradling et al, 1991), the explicit teaching of study skills (Wiltshire LEA, 1992) the use of supported self-study materials, or the dedication of professional development time to teaching and learning developments (Schon, 1983).

As with similar developments in primary schools, these initiatives are not in their own right radical departures from established practice, but are part of a continuing process of seeking to develop more responsive forms of practice. A number of features of these initiatives are worthy, therefore, of particular comment:

a. Some initiatives showed evidence of considerable creativity in respect of the issues they were addressing:

> A differentiation project sponsored by one LEA and contributed to by a number of responding schools took a refreshingly broad view of the issue and made available a wide range of teaching strategies. Instead of focusing exclusively on established approaches — differentiation by outcome, individualised work-sheets and so on — it introduced a series of sophisticated and relatively uncommon techniques — such as concept mapping, task analysis, and mastery learning. By including such techniques it made it more likely that its recommendations would be used across a range of subject areas and that they would be seen to be applicable to pupils from a wide range of ability.

b. Whereas traditionally Special Needs Co-ordinators may have seen themselves as attempting to transfer their specialist teaching strategies to mainstream colleagues, many of the teaching initiatives reported to the Project tended to have their origin firmly in non-special needs initiatives. Flexible learning, for instance, was seen by many schools as a major vehicle for developing the responsiveness of mainstream classrooms. However, its origins lie largely in the Technical and Vocational Educational Initiative of the mid-1980s rather than in developments within special education (Nash, 1993).

c. In this way, schools were addressing special needs by developing classroom strategies which were not exclusive to special education. Those strategies were, like the differentiation techniques described above, applicable to the full range of pupils. They therefore enabled teachers to assimilate the recommendations of HMI (DES, 1989a) and NCC (1989) that good practice for pupils with special needs is essentially the same as good practice for all pupils. As a result, the embedding of provision for pupils with special needs in mainstream classrooms was not seen as something which competed with provision for other pupils, but something which *enhanced* that provision.

d. There was a tendency for the *teaching* styles that were emerging to stress a more active role for the learner and hence for schools to make conscious attempts to develop particular *learning* styles:

> One school devoted an area to independent study by all pupils, and this was heavily used by those with special needs. Pupils were not 'instructed' as such, but were encouraged to identify their own targets and work autonomously using the supervising teacher, other pupils and material resources for support as necessary.
>
> In another school, the Special Needs Co-ordinator put a great deal of effort into developing learning materials for pupils with special needs to use in mainstream classrooms. However, he saw it as important that these should be *self-study* materials, and that they should be accompanied by teaching which would equip pupils with the skills to use them effectively.

Approaches such as this can be seen as attempts to increase the autonomy of pupils and reduce their dependence on teachers, thus making it easier for them to function effectively in mainstream classrooms. This has the added benefit of lessening the need for both special needs support teachers and mainstream subject teachers to make continual interventions with less able pupils.

Managing behaviour

It is not surprising that the behavioural difficulties presented by some pupils have often led teachers to seek intervention from outside the classroom by 'specialists' such as pastoral staff, special needs teachers and school counsellors. In some cases, the more problematical pupils have found themselves excluded from mainstream classrooms and ultimately from the school itself. The schools which reported to the Project, however, seemed to be addressing this issue by enhancing their own, and in particular their subject teachers', abilities to manage pupil behaviour from within their own resources. In this way, they could be seen to be embedding provision for pupils with emotional and behavioural difficulties in much the same way as they were embedding provision for learning difficulties.

One way of achieving this was through various forms of *professional development* activity. These included:

- professional development days organised in response to the Elton Report, (DES, 1989b);

- the use of systematic programmes such as BATSAC (Merrett and Wheldall, 1988) and Steps to Success (Thacker, 1982) to give teachers strategies for managing pupil behaviour.

- an extended view of professional development using peer support groups (as advocated in the Elton Report) as means of allowing teachers to share and develop their expertise collaboratively.

Schools reported that they were responding to behaviour management as a whole school issue by, for instance, *establishing working groups* to develop policy and practice in response to Elton. In one particularly interesting initiative, a school had established a multidisciplinary group to address broad pastoral issues such as drug abuse, bullying and truancy. This group was attended not only by the schools' pastoral staff but by the Special Needs Co-ordinator and by representatives of external agencies such as the Police, Psychological Services and Social Services.

Schools saw the issue of pupil behaviour as linked to the management of learning and to the creation of an appropriate *ethos* in the school. Hence, specific behaviour management initiatives were not viewed in isolation, but were set in the context of broader approaches to personal and social education and curriculum development:

One co-ordinator saw the management of behaviour not in terms of controlling disruption but of releasing and then channelling pupils' energies through appropriate teaching. In this school there was a conscious attempt to give pupils sustained positive messages about their own abilities and attainments in order to reinforce their self-esteem and release their potential as learners. This was paralleled by an approach to 'special needs' which attempted to avoid labelling or any forms of discriminatory practice, and by an approach to teaching which attempted to give all pupils as many opportunities for achievement as possible. Hence, special needs work, mainstream class

> teaching and the school's pastoral system worked in a co-ordinated way to attempt to create a highly positive ethos.

Such approaches to managing behaviour and managing learning can be seen as complementary in that they are both premised on the enhancement of the ability of mainstream schools and classrooms to respond to a greater range of pupil diversity. This is, of course, entirely consistent with the messages of the Elton Report (DES, 1989b) and, latterly, the circulars on *Pupils with Problems* (DfE, 1994b) It may be no coincidence that although many of the responding schools were in 'difficult' areas, and all had to address the issue of managing pupil behaviour, the question of discipline was not raised as a major problem by any of them.

Extended range of special needs

The enhanced ability of responding schools to cater for pupil diversity was clearly reflected in the extended range of special needs for which they actually made provision. This seemed to fall into three categories:

1. Pupils with statements

2. More able pupils

3. Individual differences

Pupils with statements

The Project found examples of schools catering for a wide range of pupils with statements, including many who in other circumstances might have been expected to attend special schools. This reflects the continuation of a trend previously reported in a number of sources (DES, 1989a, 1990). However, one interesting and novel feature is the extent to which schools were beginning to make provision for pupils with specific learning difficulties (dyslexia). In some schools such pupils constituted a substantial proportion of all pupils with statements. Although this raised some concerns about how schools might meet this demand on their resources, it also created opportunities for schools. Typically, schools had responded by seeking to meet pupils' needs substantially within the context of a differentiated mainstream curriculum, seeing withdrawal as a complement to this rather than as the principal strategy for meeting these pupils' needs. This in turn allowed schools to use whatever resources were provided through statements to support the development of a fully-differentiated curriculum. Hence support teachers, classroom assistants and resource materials tended to be used with considerable flexibility in order to benefit *all* pupils.

More able pupils

Although not constituting a special needs group in the legal sense, work with more able pupils was identified by schools as a further example of the ways they were seeking to meet needs at an individual level. This often involved using strategies such as offering pupils additional tuition or opportunities to pursue inquiry-based learning — particularly where the school had a resource centre which facilitated independent study. A particularly interesting approach was reported by one school which was collaborating with the National Association for Gifted Children in a long-term monitoring of the curriculum experiences of able pupils. This was part of an overall strategy for monitoring the quality of the curriculum for all pupils.

Individual differences

In some schools, this process of extending the range of special needs had been taken somewhat further. The detailed attention paid to the particular characteristics of individual pupils with special needs was highly valued in these schools. This led them to raise the question as to why such careful attention should not be paid to the individual characteristics of all pupils. These schools were thus coming to feel that they should operate with a concept of *individual differences*. Such a concept, they believed, was able to bring them a double benefit. On the one hand, by extending a 'special needs' approach premised on responsiveness to individual characteristics to the whole pupil population, they believed that they could enhance the quality of learning for all. On the other hand, by creating mainstream classrooms which were responsive in this way, they could reduce their dependence on segregated special needs provision and deliver more effectively the entitlement of special needs pupils to a common curricular experience:

One school had adopted a thoroughgoing individual differences perspective. It argued that all pupils were different from each other, and that such differences should be regarded as 'opportunities, not problems' — opportunities, that is, for the school to review its effectiveness in delivering an individually-responsive entitlement curriculum. Rather than focusing on pupil's negative attributes, the school regarded all its pupils as potentially successful learners, the realisation of this potential being a challenge to the skills of teachers and the quality of the school as a whole. A great deal of effort, therefore, was put into a continuous review of teaching and learning, with a particular emphasis on differentiation for all pupils, active learning, the development of flexible and sometimes individualised materials and the professional development of staff.

At the same time as the school vigorously pursued this approach, however, it exercised a good deal of caution in respect of the needs and interests of its more vulnerable pupils. It was particularly concerned that, in seeking to respond to the individual differences of *all* pupils, it did not neglect the special needs of *some*. The emphasis on differentiation was accompanied by an equal emphasis on providing a flexible and extensive system of in-class support in which a large number of staff participated. The school did not see these as mutually exclusive approaches, but rather saw in-class support as a means of developing differentiation by encouraging staff to learn from each other and providing them with the environment in which experimentation was possible.

This school's approach to individual differences is typical of the attempt to embed special needs provision which we have been describing in this section. At one level, primary and secondary schools were moving in opposite directions. The former were attempting to extricate from mainstream classroom practice an explicit set of strategies for responding to special needs, whilst the latter were seeking to 'blur the boundaries' between mainstream and special provision.

At a more fundamental level, however, schools in each phase were trying to create very similar conditions for their pupils. They were seeking to educate all children substantially within mainstream classrooms and a common entitlement curriculum. In order to do so, however, they needed teaching approaches which were flexible and responsive to the needs of individual pupils, and which were characterised by specific strategies for meeting those needs. Whilst the process of developing these strategies might focus on pupils with special needs, however, its ultimate aim was to create classrooms which were more responsive to the needs of *all* pupils.

Managing resources

Innovatory practice in secondary schools is characterised by:

the adoption of a flexible approach to managing resources in support of the learning of all pupils by: maximising resource availability; prioritising the resourcing of special needs provision; and establishing some interchangeability between those resources and mainstream resources.

In contrast to many primary schools, secondary schools have, by and large, traditionally had under their own control a small but significant level of resources for special needs — usually in the form of one or two specialist teachers, and perhaps the flexibility to involve a wider group of staff in in-class support work. The management of these resources has usually been a fairly simple matter of directing them as precisely as possible towards a selected minority of pupils.

The advantages of this approach have been:

- It has been possible to target additional resources clearly to the point of supposed need.

- Monitoring the efficient and effective use of those resources has been relatively easy.

- The protection of additional resources in the face of competing demands has been relatively straightforward.

- LEAs have (in principle, at least) been able to direct additional designated resources into schools as a means of ensuring particular levels of resources for particular children.

The developments identified by this Project, with their emphasis on viewing special needs provision as part of a broader response to individual differences, present schools with a much more complex task. First, governors and head teachers have to ensure that the resources which are allocated to pupils with special needs via statements are seen to be devoted unequivocally to their needs. Second, in most LMS formulae, there is an element which is intended to enable schools to respond effectively to the 'additional' needs of pupils without statements. Heads and governors have to ensure that this element is used effectively and that its effectiveness can be demonstrated. Third, they must carry out the first two tasks in a situation in which pupils with special needs, whether statemented or not, are functionally involved in an entitlement curriculum delivered in mainstream classrooms.

The current situation is that the SEN (Information) Regulations require schools to state in their SEN Policies how they use their resources to ensure that special educational needs are met. It is therefore important for schools to have in place clear procedures to show how they monitor their resource disposition in respect of special needs.

In the schools responding to this Project, a number of approaches were beginning to emerge in respect of these issues.

Increasing the volume of resources

As in the primary phase, a number of secondary schools responding to the Project had means of enhancing the resources at their disposal over and above those which were allocated to them via the LMS formula:

> One school was able to sustain a high level of special needs support because of the combination of a number of factors. It was fortunate in benefiting from an endowment which gave it a level of flexibility in its resourcing. It was also a very popular school with parents and was, in consequence, over-subscribed.

However, it had been able to maximise the resources available in respect of special needs by becoming, some years ago, the site for an LEA-maintained unit for pupils with moderate learning difficulties. By progressively integrating the unit into the mainstream of the school, it released its resource potential into the school as a whole. At the same time, of course, these statemented pupils gained access to the full facilities of the mainstream.

Beyond this, the school was maintained by an LEA which sought to guarantee to its schools a high degree of stability and predictability in resourcing. The head in particular felt that this enabled him to plan his resource-management more efficiently and to make equivalent internal guarantees to maintain levels of special needs provision. Moreover, the LEA encouraged schools to take responsibility for pupils with special needs and sought ways of enhancing their resourcing to this end. It had, for instance, experimented with a system of allocating additional resourcing to schools in respect of pupils who might otherwise be considered for statementing and, perhaps, placement in a special school. While this system had not been without its problems, the school nonetheless recognised the flexibility which it gave, and which enabled it to sustain a high level of special needs provision.

Finally, the school was proactive in searching for other potential resources, attempting, as the Special Needs Co-ordinator put it, to 'leech into' and 'plug in' to whatever was available. This included making use of parental support for reading and, interestingly, using support from the local Dyslexia Association for the relatively large number of pupils identified as having specific learning difficulties.

In some respects, of course, this school can be considered particularly fortunate. After all, most schools do not have the cushion of a founder's endowment. However, the school was typical of a number we studied in that it had not simply rested on its good fortune; it had, over a number of years, worked hard at maximising the resources available to it. Moreover, just as primary schools found that involvement in integration projects provided additional resources, so many secondary schools found that a commitment to special needs had resource advantages. On the one hand, work with pupils with special needs undoubtedly made particular demands on these schools' resources; on the other hand, as in the school discussed above, a commitment to special needs also brought additional resources, and those resources created a level of flexibility which could be seen to benefit all pupils.

Prioritising special needs: protection and interchange

Granted the increased autonomy which schools have experienced over recent years in respect of their management of resources, it is important to note that responding schools were characterised by a deliberate *prioritisation* of resourcing for pupils with special needs. This might take the form of a decision to appoint a co-ordinator in a senior position and to reward him or her appropriately. Alternatively, special needs provision which had been vulnerable to fluctuations in the level of funding provided through statements might be underwritten by the head and governors, thus guaranteeing a level of stability. Particularly significant was the comment of the co-ordinator at one Grant-Maintained school who reported that the school's control over its own budget had, if anything, led to an increase in special needs resourcing because, in that particular school, the governors and Senior Management Team recognised the importance of special needs.

In addition to this prioritisation and protection of special needs resourcing, responding schools were also characterised by the *flexibility* with which they managed their resources. To a certain extent, this meant thinking creatively about what might serve as a special needs resource. Hence, schools used sixth formers for support work, set up peer tutoring schemes so that pupils could support each other, or saw IT and supported self-study materials as supplements to support teaching. As one co-ordinator put it, the aim was to help pupils help themselves, and hence become less dependent on adult support.

A second tendency was for the hard and fast boundaries between 'special needs' and 'mainstream' resources to become much more permeable than has traditionally been the case. In part, this meant that designated special needs resources were used to meet a wider range of pupil learning needs. Support teaching in particular was being used not simply to support one or two less-able pupils in a class, but to respond to demands from all pupils, or to facilitate a particular curriculum development. In the same way, staff allocated to schools in respect of pupils with statements tended to work with 'their' pupil as part of a larger group and to respond to demands from a range of pupils. This in turn meant that their role became more complex, so that schools were beginning to regard them as full partners in the teaching process, and to explore ways of developing their skills.

> One school reported that the deployment of classroom assistants in this extended role offered the school greater choice in the question of whether to employ a smaller number of teachers or a larger number of assistants. This was perceived to be one of the advantages of LMS(S). Significantly, the school was not addressing this question simply in terms of which would be the cheaper option. It was trying to define carefully the boundaries between the teacher's and the assistant's role in order to decide what was the most efficient and educationally-effective way to deploy each.

This flexibility of resource-management was by no means a one-way process. Just as 'special needs' resources were deployed in support of 'mainstream' students, so 'mainstream' resources supported 'special needs' provision. In schools where there had been relatively large-scale investment in 'mainstream' curriculum development initiatives — such as flexible learning or differentiation projects — these projects were also seen to be of benefit to special needs pupils, and were often enthusiastically supported by Special Needs Co-ordinators. Similarly, where co-ordinators occupied positions of some seniority in school, they were invariably involved in initiatives which were well beyond the traditional boundaries of special needs work. Whilst this can be interpreted as a diversion of special needs resources into mainstream work, it can also be seen as the co-ordinator acquiring a seniority and status for special needs work which would not have materialised had s/he conceived the role more narrowly. This is particularly the case in the emerging role of the 'Teaching and Learning Co-ordinator' which we shall discuss below.

Resource centres

One form of interchangeable resourcing deserves particular attention. Although schools were exercising caution in their use of withdrawal as a special needs strategy, they felt a need to supplement in-class provision, and this led to some experimentation with *resource* and/or *drop-in* centres. Such centres shared with withdrawal work the strategy of working with pupils outside the classroom setting, but there the similarity ended. Drop-in centres were open access facilities, usually available outside normal lesson times, to which pupils could refer themselves or be referred as and when necessary. They typically offered support to *any* pupils who found themselves in difficulties with their work and hence were more curriculum-focused than has often been the case with withdrawal, and were certainly available to a wider range of pupils.

Resource centres took this idea one step further. Not only were they available to all pupils as a support to their normal curriculum work, but they were seen as offering extensions to that work rather than simply help to pupils who were struggling. Typically, such resource centres occupied a central location in the school — perhaps developed from the library or IT suite — were staffed by teachers or technicians throughout the timetable, contained the resources of a library together with IT and audio-visual resources, duplicate curriculum materials, and reference materials, and were accessible to pupils through self-referral or by prior arrangement with subject teachers. Although pupils with special needs could receive extra help in these settings, they were principally designed for the full range of pupils to undertake resource-based work as a normal part of their curriculum, and therefore tended to have had their origins in flexible learning initiatives.

From a special needs point of view, both drop-in and resource centres seemed to have a number of advantages:

● They allowed support to be given to special needs pupils within the context of the curriculum.

● They made such support available to a wide range of students.

● By locating support at a central point rather than within classrooms, and by providing the support when — and only when — needed, they managed available resources more cost-effectively than traditional forms of in-class support.

- By offering a service to all pupils and across the curriculum, they were able to draw on 'mainstream' resources; it is highly unlikely that the expensive equipment and materials which special needs pupils had access to in resource centres in particular could have been provided within the confines of a special needs department's suite of rooms.

Issues and possibilities

The picture that emerges in respect of resources is complex. All schools have designated funding for special needs. What seemed to distinguish the schools reporting to the Project was the extent to which they were able to identify that element and thereby to use it to establish the basis of their response to special needs. In identifying the special needs funding element these schools were able to create a sense of continuity thus allowing co-ordinators to have the confidence to plan over a longer term than the normal one year cycle. Some schools as we have indicated, were making efforts to enhance the overall level of their funding by seeking external support or arrangements with local industry or government agencies as a means of creating further flexibility in their ability to pursue their own priorities. Other schools had the good fortune to be able to call on additional resources from foundations or similar sources. In some LEAs the level of devolved funding had provided yet further degrees of freedom in which schools governors and co-ordinators could pursue innovative responses to meeting special needs.

Regardless of the level of any additional funding, what characterised the schools responding to this Project was the extent to which they had prioritised their funding for special needs. In particular, the removal of strict demarcation between 'special needs' and the 'mainstream', far from eroding what was available for special needs work, had given pupils with special needs access to the much more extensive resources available to the majority of their peers. Resources thus tended to be managed as 'resources for all' in much the same way as the curriculum was managed as a 'curriculum for all'.

However, there is a warning note to sound in respect of resources. Despite the flexibility and creativity noted above, the approaches adopted by responding schools were overwhelmingly dependent on their maintaining a level of resourcing which allowed them to provide something over and above the ordinary classroom and teacher. Without exception, they had the capability to employ specialist teachers, and/or a co-ordinator, and to supplement the mainstream classroom with additional materials and, in particular, support teaching. To a certain extent, this designated resourcing was targeted directly at identified pupils with special needs. However, in the more flexible approach operated by many of these schools, it also served to enhance the learning experiences of all pupils and — less obvious but equally important — it provided support and stimulation to mainstream subject teachers on whose whole-hearted attempts to develop a truly responsive and differentiated curriculum the schools' approaches ultimately depended. Hence, a number of co-ordinators were acutely aware of the need to deploy their 'additional' resources to make their colleagues' tasks more manageable and to secure their willing co-operation in the process of change.

It may be for this reason that some of the most interesting innovations were being undertaken not in inner city schools where the level of special need (and hence the incentive to think creatively) might be expected to be highest, but in schools with much lower levels of need and with levels of resource considered appropriate to meet that need. Certainly, one special needs inspector in an LEA which had a history of innovative approaches to special needs, expressed the opinion that mounting resource and other pressures in schools had stifled innovation in recent years.

What we have identified here may appear to be a paradox in the resourcing of special needs in responding schools. On the one hand, those schools were actively pursuing forms of provision which are more sophisticated than the simple allocation of additional resources to identified children. By crossing the boundaries between special needs and mainstream provision, they were using resources flexibly and cost-effectively, and were enabling pupils with special needs to benefit from the totality of resources in the school. Such approaches ultimately mean that the quality of special needs provision becomes less dependent on the absolute level of resourcing than on the flexibility of the school's resource-management.

On the other hand, the most creative schools also seemed to be the ones which had relatively 'generous' levels of resourcing and were dealing with manageable levels of special need. The implication would seem to be that resourcing is a factor — no doubt one among many — in the school's ability to change and develop, and that this function of resourcing is at least as important as its direct bearing on what can be provided for each pupil.

The warning note referred to above is one that was sounded by a number of respondents who reported an apprehension that the level of resourcing they had thus far enjoyed might not be sustained. They felt themselves vulnerable to changes in levels of resource provided through statements of special need, to fluctuations in their intake, and to changes in resourcing consequent upon the delegation of funding which had hitherto sustained central LEA services. There was also, in some schools, anxiety on the part of co-ordinators as to how long head teachers would continue to prioritise special needs resourcing. Resourcing special needs, of course, is always likely to remain a contentious issue, and it is difficult to determine what constitutes the 'right' level of resource. It will be interesting to see what the impact of the SEN (Information) Regulations have on this situation, since, for the first time, schools will be required to make explicit their resource-management policies, and to have their schemes to allocate resources audited by the LEA.

Managing change, managing roles

Innovatory practice in secondary schools is characterised by:

a view of effective provision for pupil diversity as requiring change and development throughout the school; such a view operationalised through strategies for promoting change, managed by a Special Needs Co-ordinator with an extended or reconstructed role within a supportive framework provided by the Senior Management Team.

Traditional forms of special needs provision in secondary schools can be seen to have had limited implications for institutional change and development. To a large extent special classes and extraction for remedial tuition were essentially self-managing and had little impact on the management of the school as a whole. Even support teaching, although it brought special needs provision into the mainstream classroom, often arose as a result of second order decisions in that it required no fundamental restructuring of timetabling or teaching.

The notion of 'embedded' special needs provision, on the other hand, is essentially about the quality of teaching and learning in every classroom. It therefore has three whole-school implications. First, it presents class teachers and subject departments across the school with the challenge of developing forms of teaching which are fully responsive to individual difference. Second, it presents governors and head teachers with the challenge of developing a policy and organisational framework which facilitates such responsiveness. Finally, for the Special Needs Co-ordinator it presents the challenge of working as a change agent with individual teachers, with subject departments and with the organisation as a whole to enable these developments to be realised in practice.

This shift in emphasis from self-contained forms of provision towards an approach which has implications for change across the school as a whole has parallels in other areas of school development. It is analogous to the management implications of a genuine whole school approach to discipline as advocated in the Elton Report (DES, 1989b), for instance, and also, we would suggest, to the implications of the school effectiveness literature (Reynolds, 1994) and of the OFSTED framework for the Inspection of Schools (OFSTED, 1992).

It is, therefore, not surprising that schools responding to the Project reported a range of strategies to bring about the changes outlined above:

Inquiry-based strategies

Just as in primary schools there was a growing use of monitoring and review procedures as the catalyst for change, so secondary schools were developing means of inquiring into various aspects of their current practice. These might indeed take the form of formal monitoring and review procedures in which evidence on the effectiveness of classroom provision was systematically gathered. This evidence then formed the basis of an agenda for internal debate which in turn led to development planning. In some cases, this debate was led by the Special Needs Co-ordinator, in others by the

Senior Management Team; in all cases, however, the debate was structured and time was allocated to it.

These procedures seemed to have two important characteristics. One was that they were collaborative and consensual, forming an accepted part of school practice and perceived to be non-threatening. The other was the use of a variety of qualitative approaches that were easily assimilated by schools and teachers; these included classroom observation, diary-keeping, staff and pupil interviews and questionnaires, and reviews of pupils' work. No school as yet had a fully-developed monitoring system matching input to outcomes, though a number of schools were clearly moving in this direction. At the time the field work for this Project was undertaken, the imminence of OFSTED inspections was beginning to generate increased interest in these approaches.

Alternatively, inquiry into practice might have much more of a research flavour. Co-ordinators often reported that they had been influenced by the experience of working for higher degrees at institutions of higher education. They spoke of the importance of action research approaches in bringing about change in their institution. In particular they saw these approaches as accessible means of taking practical action and involving a range of staff in the more effective management of teaching and learning in their classrooms.

The project-led approach to change

Some schools were seeking to stimulate widespread change by focusing on particular projects which would, they anticipated, have multiplier effects throughout the school. Some of these projects were school-based and special-needs-focused; they often formed a significant part of the role of the co-ordinator — about which we shall say more below.

As in primary schools, however, some projects were responses to external initiatives. In many cases, these were initiatives — such as TVEI, differentiation projects, Records of Achievement or Compact projects — that were not primarily targeted at pupils with special needs. Some co-ordinators saw this broader focus as an advantage. They argued that they could 'piggy-back' special needs issues on these generic teaching and learning issues. This was entirely in line with the notion that special needs should be met through developing the quality of teaching and learning for all pupils. Moreover, it encouraged schools to address special needs not as a separate — and therefore potentially marginalised — issue, but as part of the school's central concerns. In the process, it gave many co-ordinators the opportunity of injecting a special needs perspective into a wide range of whole-school initiatives.

The process of policy-formulation

A further strategy for change was the use that some schools made of their special needs policies and of the policy formulation process. Rather than seeing policies simply as a means of documenting existing procedures, secondary schools, like the primary schools we described in the previous chapter, were engaged in a continuing process of policy development which tended to involve a wide range of teachers. In particular, some policies were used to articulate a 'vision' of special needs — or, indeed, of teaching and learning generally — which could then be matched against the evidence of current practice generated by the inquiry processes outlined above and used to guide development planning:

> One school's policy began with a 'statement of philosophy' to the effect that 'All members of the school must have equality of opportunities to attain their full potential whatever their educational needs, or their background and experience.' It then moved onto a 'rationale': 'We believe that as teachers we are all teachers of students with special educational needs. Each student must be viewed as a unique individual and not merely as a member of a group'.
>
> These general statements were followed by a detailed account of policy and a set of guidelines for staff. Importantly, the policy document concluded with a set of specific 'intended outcomes', such as 'All students shall be presented with material which they can read and understand, and can respond in any way which is acceptable' or 'All students should have access to a peer group within which they can participate and learn.' Some of these outcomes had dates for achievement and thus made the review and monitoring of the policy possible.
>
> Another school had produced its policy in the form of a substantial 60 page booklet called *Accessing the Curriculum: A guide to*

> *support policy and practice*. This began with a statement of
> aims relating to the whole school, the staff, pupils, parents
> senior managers and the governing body, and then went on to
> provide guidelines for the achievement of these aims in a wide
> range of areas: staffing and resources, roles, communication,
> timetabling, collaboration and schemes of work.

As in primary schools, such policy documents could serve not only to
guide individual teachers' practice, but to bring about consistency
across the school as a whole and to promote a process of monitoring
and review which would result in the further development of both
policy and practice.

The co-ordinator as change agent

Given the developments reported above it is not surprising that the
Project identified significant developments in the role of the Special
Needs Co-ordinator. We now wish to discuss these developments in
some detail, not least because of the key role played by co-ordinators
in most schools' special needs provision.

We have seen how, in primary schools, the effectiveness of co-
ordinators has often been limited by their lack of expertise, training
and time to do the job. We have also seen how innovatory schools
were seeking to enhance the role of the co-ordinator by providing
time and enabling him/her to become involved in broad managerial
issues. In secondary schools, on the other hand, co-ordinators have
tended to have both time and some level of expertise, but they have
traditionally remained isolated from the mainstream of the school.
They tend to have been viewed by their colleagues as concerned only
with making specialist provision for a minority of pupils and have
thus been unable to engage with broader issues of teaching and
learning.

In the schools responding to the Project the co-ordinator's role was
beginning to be conceptualised somewhat differently. The Special
Needs Co-ordinator was increasingly being seen less as the provider
of support to individual pupils than as a change agent operating at
the level of both classroom practice and of whole-school policy and
organisation. Co-ordinators were thus developing a range of
strategies for engaging with colleagues' current practice as a means
of bringing about development. These strategies included:

- actively supporting and resourcing colleagues who shared their views on teaching and learning;

- openly confronting what they saw as inappropriate practice and modelling alternatives;

- offering informal advice and formal professional development to colleagues; and

- becoming involved in curriculum planning and the development of curriculum materials.

Similarly, co-ordinators had strategies for engaging with whole school and organisational issues principally by breaking out of their exclusive concern with special needs and operating across a broader front than has traditionally been the case. Hence they involved themselves in working parties, curriculum development projects and collaborative ventures with other departments across a range of issues:

One co-ordinator in an urban 11–18 comprehensive had joined the staff some ten years ago and enjoyed a high level of credibility with her colleagues. She had developed special needs provision from a reliance on traditional remedial approaches to a fuller whole-school approach based on differentiation and in-class support.

In working with individual colleagues, she placed a high priority on the opportunities afforded by the support role, seeing this as a means of helping subject teachers develop their practice rather than simply as a means of supporting individual pupils. In addition, she had established a thriving peer support group for teachers which allowed them to discuss problems and share ideas, and she had also been active in setting up regular in-service opportunities for the staff as a whole. She was a full member of the Science faculty, playing a part in all its decision-making. She valued this specialist teaching role as a means of reinforcing her credibility with colleagues. In this capacity she received in-class support from other teachers, believing that this gave her the opportunity to model appropriate roles and practice for colleagues.

She was similarly active in relation to whole-school policy and development. She was a member of the school's policy-making faculty heads' group. She had played a leading part in the school's recent review of its approach to behaviour management, and was involved with the Librarian in setting up a resource centre which was intended for the use of all pupils. This was part of a wider school thrust in the direction of differentiation, on which she was collaborating with the Senior Management Team.

More generally, she was seen by all staff — and particularly by the senior management — as a key figure in moving the school forward. She was seen as a determined, principled and proactive individual who was skilled in promoting collaborative ventures, and who had herself to be involved in all issues to do with teaching and learning.

This teacher was typical of the way co-ordinators tended to see their role as being in transition from a focus on the support of individual pupils to a broader concern with the development of a 'curriculum for all'. Indeed they experienced tension between these two perspectives and the two very different sets of activities to which they led. On the one hand co-ordinators saw curriculum development as the only way to produce a school which catered genuinely for pupil diversity; on the other hand they felt themselves continually drawn by their own and their colleagues' expectations towards intervening with individual pupils even though they recognised that this might weaken the impetus towards development in the school as a whole.

One strategy for resolving this dilemma was to define an entirely new role. This was variously entitled Teaching and Learning Co-ordinator, Head of Learning Support, or Management of Learning Leader, but all had in common a broad responsibility for enhancing the school's ability to provide effective teaching for *all* its pupils.

There were a number of interesting features of this role:

● It occupied a more senior position than that traditionally associated with that of Special Needs Co-ordinator, in some cases being located within the Senior Management Team, thus giving access to strategic decision-making processes.

- On the other hand the role was very much concerned with supporting and developing classroom practice rather than with purely administrative and logistical issues. As a result, these co-ordinators tended to spend a substantial amount of their time in their own and their colleagues' classrooms.

- The role carried with it a wide-ranging brief which linked together previously disparate areas such as appraisal, professional development, curriculum development and provision for individual pupils.

- As such the role was not constrained by existing organisational structures such as departments and therefore enabled the co-ordinator to manage issues across the school as a whole which might otherwise have remained untouched. In particular, the existence of the role defined teaching and learning as *the* central whole school issue which demands explicit and coherent management.

- Some Senior Management Teams reported that they saw the creation of the role as a means of bringing about significant change. The implication was that the role occupant was often given considerable freedom in identifying and addressing development needs in the school.

- In line with the strategies for change identified in the previous section, the occupants of this role tended to be responsible for some sort of monitoring and inquiry processes increasing the flow of high quality information as the basis of development planning.

The relationship between this role and the traditional Special Needs Co-ordinator's role is worthy of further analysis. Three patterns were apparent.

1. Organic growth

    The Special Needs Co-ordinator might extend his or her role to the point at which he or she became a *de facto* Teaching and Learning Co-ordinator whilst still retaining day to day special needs responsibilities.

2. Division of labour

    A Teaching and Learning Co-ordinator might be appointed as line manager of Special Needs Co-ordinator. This had the effect of defining the latter's role in a much more circumscribed traditional way than in many other responding schools.

3. Radical transformation

One school dispensed entirely with the Special Needs Co-ordinator's role, adopting the radical stance that a Teaching and Learning Co-ordinator managing effective provision for all was *ipso facto* managing provision for special needs pupils.

Both Teaching and Learning Co-ordinators and Special Needs Co-ordinators developing a wider role seemed to share a number of personal and professional characteristics.

- They tended to have a diversity of experience not solely restricted to the mainstream school special needs area. Two of the Special Needs Co-ordinators in the case study schools, for instance, had experience of managing unit provision for pupils with statements; another had been an LEA advisory teacher. Teaching and Learning Co-ordinators in particular might be drawn from mainstream curriculum areas.

- This diversity of experience was reflected in a breadth of vision enabling them to see broader issues and principles. Hence, they tended to be able to articulate a coherent view of their role, to relate it to broader issues in education, to understand its place within the micro-politics of the school, and to talk in terms of the inter-relationship of their work with wider issues of professional and organisational development.

- This breadth of vision was attributable in part to their extended professional networks, which helped them guard against insularity:

> One co-ordinator had founded a branch of the National Association of Special Educational Needs as a means of strengthening regional networks. A second was active in delivering INSET at a local higher education college as a means of learning from other schools as well as sharing her own experiences with them. Others commented that their studies for higher degrees had been the crucial factors in broadening their perception of special needs.

- They appeared to have in many cases excellent working relationships with their colleagues which were important in allowing them to discharge their extended roles effectively. It was evident from the comments of their colleagues in many schools that they tended to enjoy a high level of professional credibility and were adept at using this to gain support for change and development. For this reason they were often seen as personally helpful and supportive even when the changes in practice which they were promoting were seen as somewhat threatening.

- A number of them reported that they had experienced periods of turbulence when staff resistance to change was particularly high. They had nonetheless been sustained by a strong sense of justice and clear professional values to which they felt themselves to be fundamentally committed.

It is perhaps worth noting at this point that the Project identified three schools which had taken the processes described above further still. Not only had the Special Needs Co-ordinator disappeared, but neither had a Teaching and Learning Co-ordinator post been established in its place. Instead the schools devolved responsibilities to existing structures (such as subject departments and pastoral teams) and handed oversight of 'individual differences' issues to representative groups of staff working collaboratively.

In so doing, the schools might be seen to have lost the impetus that the presence of a co-ordinator with overall responsibility might have given them. There was also a risk that the absence of a single clearly-identified advocate would make it less likely that the interests of children with special needs would be protected effectively. On the other hand, these schools were characterised by a high level of commitment by staff, heads and governors to the prioritisation of special needs issues and the protection of special needs pupils. Moreover, as one of the schools argued, embedding responsibility in existing structures avoided the danger of special needs being seen as 'someone else's problem'. It will be interesting to monitor how these schools respond to the requirement in the SEN (Information) Regulations that all schools have a named person. Clearly, it will be vital for schools to demonstrate that all their staff are working to a common set of principles, procedures and practices. For secondary schools this may not be easy to achieve without the action of an actual co-ordinator. Smaller schools may evolve other mechanisms to achieve this end and there will be a need to monitor such developments. Whatever systems are ultimately developed schools and governors are charged of course with the responsibility of ensuring that the provision they make for pupils with special needs meets the principles laid down in the Code of Practice and the SEN (Information) Regulations.

Senior managers as managers of change

It will be evident from what we have said in preceding sections that a feature of responding schools was the key role played by senior management, and in particular the Headteacher, in structuring and enabling innovatory forms of provision. As special needs issues become increasingly identified with broader issues of teaching and learning, so the boundary between the responsibilities of the co-ordinator and of senior management becomes increasingly fluid.

Many of the schools responding to the Project were fortunate in having head teachers who were at the very least prepared to grant co-ordinators a considerable degree of autonomy and to resource them in terms of staffing and non-timetabled time to play a significant role across the school. In most of these schools, however, senior managers were proactive beyond this minimum level. In particular they tended to:

- regard the co-ordinator as a major resource at their disposal for bringing about change in the school that was both far-reaching and was also effective at the level of classroom practice — something which they themselves by virtue of their 'distance' from the classroom could not readily achieve;

- appoint teachers to co-ordinator posts who were extended professionals able to operate with a high level of autonomy, to think strategically and to communicate effectively with their colleagues;

- give teaching and learning issues, including special needs, a high priority within the school, particularly in terms of resource allocation.

More fundamentally, senior managers tended to locate the changes which co-ordinators were seeking to bring about within an overarching strategy for change and development in the school as a whole.

Where the co-ordinator appeared to have the greatest impact, change was planned strategically by senior managers and was guided by an all-embracing 'vision' of what the school might be, which was articulated by the head in particular but was beginning to be shared more widely across the school.

Professional development

> **Innovatory practice in secondary schools is characterised by:**
>
> a view of the professional expertise of all staff as an essential resource in the school's response to pupil diversity, to be enhanced through school-centred professional development strategies.

Whereas professional development in the field of special educational needs has traditionally taken the form of the training of specialist staff in 'special needs' skills, the model of provision that has been identified by this Project requires a somewhat different approach. Since provision is made by all staff, professional development must likewise be extended to include all staff; and since special needs provision is 'embedded' in mainstream classroom provision, so the emphasis must be on enhancing and extending the skills which mainstream teachers *already* have, rather than on trying to equip them with a new and entirely different set of skills.

It is not surprising, therefore, that schools reported to the Project professional development strategies which were heavily focused on the development of mainstream teachers' skills *in situ*. In this respect secondary schools closely paralleled developments in primary schools though their size and complexity led them in some cases to evolve more highly systematised approaches. As in primary schools, much INSET was school-centred in being located in the school and focused on teachers' day to day concerns. However, secondary schools had more flexibility to involve external providers particularly from higher education as well as making use of the co-ordinator as INSET deliverer. In either case it was notable that 'special needs INSET' was viewed as part of a clearly-articulated and long-term programme of development and that it embraced more general teaching concerns such as differentiation, flexible learning, assessment and discipline.

As we have already seen, many Special Needs Co-ordinators saw professional development as a major function of their role. Some of them were operating with a sophisticated notion of professional development in which continuing routine interactions with colleagues were seen as being even more important than high-profile events. They saw in-class support as an opportunity for special needs teachers to model teaching strategies, and the participation of mainstream teachers in a support role as an important strategy for deepening those teachers' understandings. As in primary schools, there was a sense that the staff as a whole constituted a pool of potentially untapped expertise. The aim therefore was to encourage teachers and departments to share their expertise in order to cross-fertilise each other's work.

This same notion to a certain extent underpinned the use of research and inquiry techniques noted above. Schools appeared to be operating on the assumption that teachers could become effective problem-solvers in respect of special needs, given a framework such as action research or quality assurance which could help them focus their skills. Co-ordinators expressed reluctance to act, in the words of one policy statement, as 'experts able to provide instant and simple solutions', preferring instead to think in terms of 'empowering people'.

Collaborative working

Innovatory practice in secondary schools is characterised by:

the establishment of collaborative working arrangements within the school, particularly between the special needs 'facility' and the mainstream of the school in order that subject teachers might be effective in making provision for all their pupils; in some cases, strategies for drawing upon resources external to the school in support of the school's approach.

The traditional organisation of secondary schools around subject departments and separate academic and pastoral systems has made the process of collaboration problematical. Similarly, in terms of external relations, the ability of many secondary schools to sustain their own forms of special needs provision has made them relatively independent of the LEA and its services, and has militated against the development of collaborative arrangements.

The notion of embedding special needs provision in the mainstream, however, seems to necessitate a more collaborative approach both internally and externally. If special needs issues can no longer be hived off as the exclusive responsibility of some small part of the school or education system, and if they are seen as closely linked to issues of teaching and learning for all pupils, then there are sound reasons why teachers, schools and services should work more closely together.

Internal collaboration

It was characteristic of responding schools that they had developed systems and structures which allowed them to link their special needs teachers and departments more closely with other areas of the school. One strategy was for schools to establish steering groups or liaison committees which were drawn from subject departments, led by the Special Needs Co-ordinator, and which served the purpose of strengthening collaboration between the special needs facility and the rest of the school. In some cases, these groups simply served to increase the information flow in respect of pupils with special needs. In other cases, however, they had responsibility for taking managerial decisions such as the allocation of support teaching. In one school, these 'link teachers' were actually appointed jointly to a subject department and the Special Needs Team.

Even where there was no managerial group as such, there was a tendency to involve mainstream teachers in the management of special needs resources. In some schools, for instance, support teaching was allocated to a greater or lesser extent not according to the Special Needs Co-ordinator's judgement of where the greatest special needs might lie, but in response to bids submitted by subject departments specifying the benefits they expected from such additional resourcing. In other schools, subject departments were at least in part responsible for providing support from within their own staffing. In one school there was a 'payback' system whereby a teacher who had been the beneficiary of in-class support would later spend some time as a support teacher. The possibility was raised in this school of a system of internal secondments which would allow subject teachers to spend a term working as special needs teachers in order to increase cross-fertilisation.

The extended role of the Special Needs Co-ordinator, which we described in a preceding section, is of course itself a significant mechanism for promoting collaboration. By actively pursuing a process of embedding special needs, working closely with colleagues in their classrooms and across a range of whole-school issues, co-ordinators were effectively breaking down the barriers that had previously kept them isolated. This was typified by the importance many co-ordinators attached to retaining a subject-teaching commitment alongside their special needs work, thus demonstrating the close relationship between mainstream and special needs teaching.

This enhancement of collaboration within the school had the consequence that role boundaries could become somewhat blurred. Co-ordinators reported that it might, for instance, be far from clear whether they or the year tutor should take the lead in particular cases. Similarly the demarcation of responsibilities between Curriculum Deputies and Teaching and Learning Co-ordinators tended to be uncertain. However, in many schools, the high level of credibility and trust accorded to the co-ordinator and the collaborative culture established within the school made this a strength rather than a weakness. Teachers were able to work in teams drawing upon each other's expertise to fashion a flexible response to pupils' difficulties. When it was suggested to one co-ordinator that her role overlapped with that of year tutors, her reply was typical: 'I've never really thought about it like that. It doesn't matter who does it, so long as it gets done!'.

External collaboration

Many schools reported that they were seeking to mirror the growth of internal collaboration with equivalent forms of collaboration with other networks. This was particularly true of schools which had developed, perhaps with LEA facilitation, some form of clustering arrangement with other institutions. The 'family' system of clustering referred to in the chapter on primary schools, for instance, was also perceived as beneficial at secondary level, and for similar reasons.

As in primary schools also, there were signs of reconstituted partnerships with local authorities and their services. Schools had opted into LEA sponsored projects which were less concerned with promulgating policy than with networking the expertise of a number of schools around a common theme. Elsewhere, schools were making use of LEA services in a flexible and imaginative way:

> One school was using some of its allocated time from the educational psychological service in a non traditional way. Rather than using her in the traditional role of assessor of individual children's needs, the school asked her to carry out an evaluation of its special needs provision. In particular, she was reviewing the role of a recently-designated Teaching and Learning Co-ordinator, and was facilitating groups of teachers who were looking at teaching and learning styles and the management of pupil behaviour. Some of her work with these groups was based on direct observations of teaching which she had been invited to carry out. As a professional who was independent of the school but who was also developing a detailed knowledge of its operation, she was able to act as a bridge between the staff and the senior management of the school.

In other cases collaboration was less formalised but nonetheless constituted a positive force. Co-ordinators, for instance, reported that they appreciated the opportunity to network with their counterparts in other schools, and were particularly keen to learn through this Project of developments elsewhere in the country. In one authority, a number of schools participated in an issue-based group which sought to clarify and refine the direction in which the role of the special needs co-ordinator might develop.

Summary

The principal concern of the innovatory secondary schools that we have studied is to 'embed' their special needs provision in mainstream classrooms and a common entitlement curriculum. They are seeking to break down the traditional barriers between the sorts of learning experiences that are offered to most children and the discrete forms of practice and provision that have been offered to pupils with special needs. This is leading them to develop styles of teaching and learning that are flexible and responsive to the needs of all pupils and hence to explore the implications of the concept of 'individual differences'.

In order to do this, they are taking advantage of their increased autonomy to manage their resources flexibly in support of the learning of all. They are seeing the expertise of the staff as a whole as a key resource to be managed and are focusing on ways of promoting both professional development and staff collaboration. In particular, they see the development of flexible and responsive forms of practice as requiring change at both an individual and organisational level. The Special Needs Co-ordinator has a key part to play in this process, and is beginning to operate in an extended role which is not confined to the support of individual pupils with special needs. Rather s/he increasingly acts as promoter and facilitator of change in respect of teaching and learning issues as they affect all pupils.

4: Themes and issues in innovatory provision and practice

Thus far, data from primary and secondary schools have been presented separately in order to capture the significant but sometimes subtle differences between provision in those two phases. However, it is important to determine whether primary and secondary schools are in fact moving in different directions, or whether their varying practices are actually underpinned by a common understanding of special needs. In order to do this, it will be useful to compare and contrast the principal features of innovatory provision in each phase. Figure 1 (see P.74) therefore summarises the findings from primary and secondary schools.

Towards a common approach?

Clearly, there are some significant differences in emphasis and many differences of detail between primary and secondary schools. However, set side by side in this way, it is apparent that there is also broad similarity between the emerging approaches in primary and secondary schools. These approaches appear to be underpinned by a common understanding of how schools can and should respond to pupils with special needs. It may be useful to delineate the main features of that understanding.

> At its heart is the goal of *embedding provision for pupils with special needs within ordinary classrooms and an entitlement curriculum*. The corollary of this is that teachers within those classrooms are able to deploy *a repertoire of strategies which allow them to respond to a wide range of pupil diversity*. This central purpose is supported in four ways:
>
> 1. The creative deployment of all the school's resources in support of the learning of all its pupils.
>
> 2. The promotion of organisational development to enable the school to respond to pupil diversity.
>
> 3. The development of the professional expertise of all staff as facilitators of learning.
>
> 4. Support for individual teachers by the establishment of collaborative working arrangements within and beyond the school.

Figure 1 Principal features of innovatory provision and practice in primary and secondary schools

PRIMARY SCHOOLS	SECONDARY SCHOOLS
Explicating teaching and learning practices	**Embedding provision for pupil diversity**
A growing repertoire of explicated strategies for teaching and learning, developed within and implemented by the school, enabling all pupils, including those with special needs, to learn effectively within the context of an entitlement curriculum.	Strategies for embedding provision for the full range of pupil diversity within ordinary classrooms and in the context of an entitlement curriculum, underpinned by notions of individual differences and supporting the learning of all pupils.
Resource management	**Resource management**
An approach in which the school takes responsibility for managing its own resources flexibly in support of the learning of all pupils by: maximising resource availability; identifying and prioritising special needs resources, and establishing some interchangeability between those resources and mainstream resources.	The school adopts a flexible approach to managing its resources in support of the learning of all pupils by: maximising resource availability; prioritising the resourcing of special needs provision; and establishing some interchangeability between those resources and mainstream resources.
Managing change, managing roles	**Managing change, managing roles**
A view of effective provision for pupil diversity as requiring change and development throughout the school; such a view operationalised through strategies for promoting change, managed by the headteacher but involving the special needs co-ordinator in an extended role.	A view of effective provision for pupil diversity as requiring change and development throughout the school; such a view operationalised through strategies for promoting change, managed by a special needs co-ordinator with an extended or reconstructed role within a supportive framework provided by the Senior Management Team.
Professional development	**Professional development**
A view of the professional expertise of *all* staff as an essential resource in the school's response to pupil diversity, to be enhanced through school-centred professional development strategies.	A view of the professional expertise of *all* staff as an essential resource in the school's response to pupil diversity, to be enhanced through school-centred professional development strategies.
Collaborative working	**Collaborative working**
The establishment of collaborative working arrangements both within and beyond the school in order that schools and teachers might be more effective in making provision for all their pupils, thus becoming less reliant on external interventions.	The establishment of collaborative working arrangements within the school, particularly between the special needs 'facility' and the mainstream of the school, in order that subject teachers might be more effective in making provision for all their pupils. In some cases, strategies for drawing upon resources external to the school in support of the school's approach.

At the beginning of this book, we suggested that schools faced four key challenges in respect of special needs in the 1990s: ensuring access to a common curriculum; meeting the particular needs of individual children; taking responsibility for managing their own resources; and doing each of these in the context of greater public accountability. Readers may now wish to consider the extent to which the features of innovatory provision and practice outlined above are likely to enable schools to meet these challenges. It is our view that special needs provision in mainstream schools will constantly require review. However, the schools whose work we have reported here have much to offer by way of identifying directions which other schools may wish to explore.

In order to facilitate this exploration, therefore, we now propose to restate the key features and assumptions which innovatory schools have adopted. We also wish to suggest some considerations which other schools may wish to take into account when reviewing their own practice and provision.

a) Embedded provision and clarified and codified practice

Key assumption:

It is possible for schools to articulate teaching and learning practices which enable mainstream teachers to make effective provision for a wide range of pupil diversity within the context of an entitlement curriculum.

Considerations:

- Such practices should see learning as a process which has to be managed explicitly and proactively for *all* pupils. In so doing it meets the needs of pupils whether they have statements of special needs, non statemented special needs, or the needs of any individual learner.

- These practices do not require a new 'technology' of teaching, but the wider deployment of strategies — such as flexible learning, peer tutoring, individual programming and collaborative group work — which are already to hand.

- The making explicit and wider deployment of these strategies is not a task for teachers working in isolation. Teachers need to work in teams and partnerships and to be supported by whole-school resources, policies and approaches.

● Significant amongst these supportive partnerships is collaboration with colleagues who can make available the expertise and approaches associated with special needs work.

b) Resources and special needs

Key assumption:

The flexible and creative deployment of resources by schools enables them to become effective in making provision for a wide range of pupil diversity.

Considerations:

● By seeing special needs provision as part of wider provision for all pupils, schools can use both 'special' and 'mainstream' resources to maximum advantage.

● On the other hand, this 'interchange' of resources should not be equated with the seepage of resources away from children with special needs; schools need to establish priorities for making provision for children with special needs.

● In the context of local management, schools can be proactive in maximising the resources available to them and in deploying those resources in ways which have maximal developmental effect.

● Schools need a sufficient flexibility in resources to construct an approach for supporting the learning of all pupils. Local management of schools (or in the case of GM schools, the annual maintenance grant) gives schools overall flexibility within their budgets. Schools need to describe in their written policies how they employ their funds for special needs provision — for example to introduce degrees of freedom beyond the one teacher — one class model of provision, which would give them access to teachers with expertise and experience in special needs provision. This may encourage the development of 'clustering' in the ways we have outlined above.

c) Roles and the management of change

Key assumption:

Effective special needs provision requires change and development throughout the school, led by a co-ordinator and actively promoted by senior management.

Considerations:

- Managing special needs provision should be seen as part of the wider task of managing the school's educational effectiveness, and is thus central to the concerns of senior managers.

- The promotion of effectiveness requires the school to deploy a range of developmental strategies at individual teacher, teaching team, and institutional levels.

- The role of the Special Needs Co-ordinator may well need to be extended to embrace these wider managerial issues. In some cases, the co-ordinator may be responsible to, or even become, a senior member of staff whose primary task is the promotion of effective teaching and learning throughout the school.

- The alignment of special needs issues with other whole-school issues means that senior managers have a key role to play in actively promoting development in the school. The appointment or designation of a Special Needs Co-ordinator alone does not mark the extent of senior managers' responsibilities in this area.

d) Professional development

Key assumption:

The professional expertise of all staff as facilitators of learning is an essential resource in the school's response to pupil diversity.

Considerations:

- Since professional expertise is a key resource, schools need to have explicit strategies for developing that expertise.

- These strategies need to relate to all staff, not just 'special needs teachers'.

- Such strategies are aimed at enhancing the ability of the school as a whole to respond to student diversity rather than simply at equipping a minority of staff with special needs expertise. Accordingly, they need to focus on how staff work as a team in their day-to-day context on the problems presented by diversity. They need, in other words, to be school-centred problem-solving strategies.

- Since effective teaching and learning for pupil diversity appears not to require a new technology of teaching, it is probable that much professional development will focus on the enhancement of existing teaching skills and strategies.

- For all of these reasons, professional development strategies will need to range beyond traditional models of INSET delivery and will be largely managed and provided from the school's own resources.

- On the other hand, the key roles played by Senior Managers and Special Needs Co-ordinators imply the need for specific forms of training for them, and, in the case of co-ordinators in particular, for networks of professional support.

e) Collaborative working

Key assumption:

Schools are enabled to cater for pupil diversity by the establishment of collaborative working arrangements both within and beyond the school.

Considerations:

- Catering for pupil diversity should be regarded as the responsibility not of individual teachers working in isolation, but of the school operating as a flexible unit. Accordingly, schools need to develop explicit strategies and structures for facilitating genuine teamwork between teachers. In particular, there need to be structures and strategies which enable mainstream class and subject teachers to work collaboratively with special needs specialists.

- In order to extend their own ability to cater for pupil diversity, schools need to develop strategies for drawing upon a wide range of external resources, and, in particular, for working collaboratively with other schools and with the LEA and its services.

● Schools need to adopt a proactive role in developing partnerships with parents and to examine ways in which the resources of the community can be fully utilised for the benefit of all pupils.

5: Innovation, evolution and the changing context

The 1993 Act and the Code of Practice

Our research was conducted over the period when the 1993 Education Act was in preparation. The schools we worked with, therefore, were operating in a different legislative framework from that which now forms the context for special needs provision. The question inevitably arises therefore as to the extent of the congruence between the developments we have reported and the new legislative framework. It is beyond the scope of this book to undertake a detailed analysis of the 1993 Act and its accompanying Code of Practice and Circulars. Nonetheless, it may be useful to draw attention to some of the interesting parallels that emerge.

In many respects, the approach to special needs in the 1993 Act, and in particular in the Code of Practice, is firmly rooted in the philosophy of the 1981 Education Act and, before that, of the Warnock Report. It remains fully committed to the notion that some children's educational needs are 'special', that those needs should be assessed on an individual basis, and that special measures need to be taken to meet those needs. Moreover, some special needs are such that they may well require additional resources and legal protection.

However, the new legislation constitutes a significant reinterpretation of the principles of the 1981 Act in the light of the new context created by the 1988 Education Reform Act. The focus in the 1981 Act was very much on the local education authority in that it is the LEA which has the responsibility to assess, resource and provide for special needs. The changed relationships between schools and LEAs which the intervening years have brought about, however, have given schools an increased level of autonomy and, in particular, have given them much more direct control over the management of their resources. In consequence, the single locus of responsibility envisaged by the 1981 Act has required some reconceptualisation. Thus the new legislation seeks to distribute responsibility for special needs much more evenly between LEAs and schools.

The 1993 Act and the Code of Practice will in future require all schools to accept a level of responsibility for special needs provision which is commensurate with their increased autonomy. Many of the developments we have reported above, however, can be seen as instances of schools acknowledging such responsibilities and seeking to work out their implications in advance of the formulation of the new legislative framework. Although, therefore, we would not claim that the developments we have reported prefigure the Code in every respect, we would argue that there are some central features of innovatory practice and provision which indicate promising ways forward for schools as they seek to come to terms with the new situation.

Readers will no doubt wish to consider the ways in which developments reported under 'Teaching and Learning' can be used to help them review their own school's strategies under the Code's staged assessment and provision procedures. Similarly, we would suggest that our findings on policy development (see, for example, pages 12–13, 28–29 and 59–60) might be helpful to schools seeking to develop their special needs policy. There are many other instances where, we believe, schools may find the emerging practice which we have reported helpful in thinking through the implications of the Code. However, we wish briefly to highlight two points in particular.

The role of the Special Needs Co-ordinator

The Code of Practice has given a renewed importance to the role of the Special Needs Co-ordinator. For many schools, with long-established, well-trained and highly-effective co-ordinators, this will not present any problems. However, two concerns do seem to be emerging in some quarters.

The first, particularly (though not exclusively) characteristic of primary schools, is the issue of how time can be found to enable the co-ordinator to carry out his/her duties. Our findings do not suggest any easy answers to this problem, but they do suggest that some primary schools have been able to sustain a powerful and effective co-ordinator's role. Given sufficient prioritisation of special needs, the creative management of resources, and the realisation that special needs issues are linked more generally to issues of teaching and learning for all, then the co-ordinator's role becomes not simply viable but integral to the development of the school.

The second issue relates to the concerns amongst some co-ordinators that the Code will divert their energies into an essentially administrative function. Again, there are no simple answers to this dilemma, and co-ordinators will need to manage their time with great care. Nonetheless, it would appear that many co-ordinators were able to reconcile a detailed and effective system of assessment, record-keeping and individual programming with a broader role in organisational development. Co-ordinators may need to give some thought to the appropriate balance between these aspects of their role. In particular it may be the case that time invested in developing effective practice and systems throughout the school will be repaid by a reduced demand for interventions at an individual level and hence a reduced administrative load. In the language of the Code itself, co-ordinators may need to think about the distribution of their effort between the development of routine practice in ordinary classrooms at stage 1, and the more individualised (and time-consuming) interventions at stages 2 and 3.

The role of the governing body

Given the growing autonomy of schools, it is not surprising that the 1993 Act and the Code of Practice stress the central role to be played by schools' governing bodies. It is the governors' responsibility to determine the school's general policy and approach to special needs. It is clear that in many schools governors will play an active role in the direction of special needs policy, and this will require governors, headteachers and special needs co-ordinators to think through the ways in which they relate to each other and carry out their different but interdependent responsibilities.

In a number of schools, some evidence of this new relationship was beginning to emerge. Some schools, for instance, already had in place a governor who had specific responsibilities for special needs issues. This was particularly significant in those schools where the designated governor made a point of informing themselves about special needs issues in general and about the detail of special needs provision in their school in particular. In some cases, these governors were themselves parents of children with special needs or had a particular background in special needs work; in all cases, however, they went out of their way to talk to the special needs staff and to see for themselves the school's special needs work in action. In return, headteachers and Special Needs Co-ordinators made sure that governors were given detailed information about special needs provision, and were keen to discuss with them both the successes and problems of their work.

It is entirely understandable that some Special Needs Co-ordinators might have anxieties that the changing role of governors might threaten their professional autonomy. Clearly, this relationship will need careful handling. In these schools, however, both the co-ordinators and the governors described a process of growth in mutual understanding fostered by an open exchange of information and ideas. Indeed, some co-ordinators saw the designated governor as an important ally in protecting and prioritising special needs issues and resources.

Innovation or Evolution?

It will be evident from the foregoing that we believe there are many points at which the guidance of the Code of Practice and the sorts of innovatory developments we have reported coincide with one another. However, we have argued that the Code is very much predicated upon the principles and procedures which informed the Warnock Report and the 1981 Education Act. This inevitably begs the question as to how genuinely 'innovatory' our innovatory schools are. Have they developed a radically new form of special needs provision and set of special needs practices, or are they simply adapting the tradition of the whole school approach to a somewhat changed external environment?

Throughout this book and, indeed, the whole of our Project, we have been content to operate with a somewhat loosely-defined notion of innovation. As researchers, we were looking for practice and provision that was 'interestingly different', but, in order to capture as many examples as possible, we were content to let schools, LEAs and other informants report to us whatever *they* chose to regard as innovatory. Many readers may therefore feel that some of the practice we have included does not accord with their own definitions of what is innovatory, and, indeed, a number of responding schools — particularly in the primary phase — were highly reticent about applying the term to their work.

Having analysed the data from these schools, however, we now feel we are in a position to give a retrospective definition of what innovatory means in the context of mainstream schools' special needs provision in the 1990s. We wish to argue that *innovation should not be sought in terms of the range and nature of the forms of special needs provision or the sets of special needs practices that were emerging in these schools*. At the outset of our work, we had wondered whether we might not uncover dramatically new forms of meeting special needs. In reality, however, we suggest that many of the surface features of what we found could equally well have been found in the previous decade — though these features may have become more developed and widespread in the intervening years.

Our analysis leads us to believe that there is a different way of identifying innovation in schools. *Instead of looking at each form of provision and practice singly and asking how different it is from what has gone before, it is possible to examine the totality of the school's approach to special needs and to analyse it in terms of its underpinning principles and purposes.* This is what we have sought to do in presenting the features of provision and practice which our research has uncovered in terms of major *themes*. These themes, we would suggest, point towards a very different understanding of special needs which can rightly be called 'innovatory'.

Central to this new understanding is a commitment to a dual entitlement — entitlement to participation in a common curriculum and a shared learning environment; and entitlement to flexible and sensitive responses to individual needs and characteristics. Schools could see these two entitlements as in conflict with each other — that a common curriculum demands the abandonment of individual responsiveness, and that individual responsiveness must take place outside the common curriculum. What innovatory schools have succeeded in doing is resolving this potential contradiction. They have sought to reconstruct the relationship between curriculum and individual need by seeing that if a common curriculum is taught with sufficient flexibility and with due regard to individual need it becomes the most powerful means for meeting the educational needs of all children.

In order to achieve this, therefore, they have ceased to think of special needs provision as something that either takes place outside the curriculum (and classroom) or is imported into the classroom in the form of support teaching. Instead, they have come to see special needs provision as 'built into', or embedded, in the very routines that constitute ordinary classroom practice. In so doing, they have considerably enhanced their ability to respond to *all* needs and characteristics. Doing this has not required the invention of radically new practices, but rather the ability to see new potential in established practices and new ways of integrating them in order to serve new purposes. It is this shift in thinking, we would argue, which characterises innovatory schools and makes their approach something distinctive in the field of special needs.

Given the diversity of all schools and, in particular, the very different organisational forms of primary and secondary schools, it is not surprising that this commitment to shared principles has not led to a uniformity of provision. Schools have very different starting points and work in very different contexts; their commitment to entitlement and responsiveness, therefore, will lead them to different resolutions. Moreover, the process of change itself will be different in each case. In some schools, therefore, we found sudden breaks with the past leading to what might be considered radical forms of provision. In others we found much more evolutionary change leading to forms whose surface features seemed quite conservative but where the effect of the totality of those features was to deliver the dual entitlements we described above.

We suggest therefore that schools should not seek in this research for a single *blueprint* for change. They must inevitably find their own way from their own starting points. However, we would suggest that the work of innovatory schools maps out certain possibilities that all schools would do well to consider.

References

Alexander, R. (1992) *Policy and Practice in Primary Education*. London: Routledge.

Bines, H. (1986) *Redefining Remedial Education*. London: Croom Helm.

Clark, C., Dyson, A. and Millward, A. (1990) 'Evolution or Revolution: dilemmas in the post ERA management of special educational needs by local authorities'. *Oxford Review of Education*, Vol. 16, 3, pp. 279–293.

Clay, M. (1993) *Reading Recovery: a guidebook for teachers in training*. London: Heineman.

DES (1989a) *A Survey of Pupils with Special Educational Needs in Ordinary Schools*. A Report by HM Inspectorate. London: HMSO

DES (1989b) *Discipline in Schools* (The Elton Report). London: HMSO.

DES (1989c) *From Policy to Practice*. London: HMSO.

DES (1978) *Special Educational Needs* (The Warnock Report), London: HMSO.

DES (1990) *Education Observed: Special Needs Issues*. A Survey by HM Inspectorate. London: HMSO.

DFE (1994a) *Code of Practice on the Identification and Assessment of Special Educational Needs*. London: DFE.

DFE (1994b) *Pupils with Problems* (Circulars 8–13/94). London: DFE.

Dessent, T. (1987) *Making the Ordinary School Special*. Lewes: Falmer Press.

Dyson, A. (1990) 'Effective learning consultancy: A future role for special needs coordinators?' *Support for Learning*, 5, 3, pp. 116–127.

Dyson, A. (1991) 'Rethinking roles, rethinking concepts: Special needs teachers in mainstream schools'. *Support for Learning*, 6, 2, pp. 51–60.

Dyson, A. and Gains, C. (1993) *Rethinking Special Needs in Mainstream Schools: Towards the year 2000*. London: David Fulton.

Dyson, A., Millward, A. and Skidmore, D. (1994) 'Beyond the whole school approach: An emerging model of special needs provision in secondary schools'. *British Educational Research Journal* 20, 3, pp. 301–317.

Egan, G. (1973) *Face to Face: Small Group Experience and Interpersonal Growth*. Monterey, Ca.: Brooks-Cole.

Eraut, M., Nash, C., Fielding, M. and Attard, P. (1991) *Flexible Learning in Schools*. London: Employment Department.

Gilbourn, D., Nixon, J. and Ruddock, J. (1993) *Dimensions of Discipline in Secondary Schools*. London: HMSO.

Hanko, G. (1985) *Special Needs in Ordinary Classrooms*. London: Blackwell.

Hart, S. (1986) 'In-class support teaching: Tackling Fish'. *British Journal of Special Education* 13, 2, pp. 57–58.

Lunt, I., Evans, J., Norwich, B. and Weddell, K. (1994) *Working Together: Inter School Collaboration for Special Needs*. London: David Fulton.

Lunzer, E. & Gardiner, K. (Eds) (1979) *The Effective Use of Reading*. London: Heinemann.

Merrett, F. and Wheldall, K. (1988) *BATSAC Training Package*. Birmingham: Positive Products.

Moore, J. (1993) 'How will the 'self managing' school manage?' in A. Dyson and C. Gains. (Eds.) *Rethinking Special Needs in Mainstream Schools: Towards the Year 2000*. London: David Fulton.

Mosley. J. (1991) *All Round Success — Practical Ideas to Enhance Self Esteem Within the Classroom*. Trowbridge: Wiltshire LEA.

Mosley, J. (1988) 'Dramatherapy: Helping children with behaviour problems'. *Maladjustment and Therapeutic Education*, 6, 2, pp. 120–126.

Nash, C. (1993) 'Flexible Learning'. In A. Dyson and C. Gains (Eds.) *Rethinking Special Needs in Mainstream Schools: Towards the Year 2000*. London: David Fulton.

National Curriculum Council (1989) *Curriculum Guidance 2: A Curriculum for All*. York: NCC.

Norwich, B. and Daniels, H. (1992) 'Support from the team'. Managing Schools Today, 1, 6, pp. 30–31.

OFSTED (1994) *The Handbook for School Inspection*. London: HMSO.

Peter, M. (Ed) (1992) *Differentiation: Ways Forward*. Stafford: NASEN. Reprinted from *British Journal of Special Education*, 19, 1.

Reynolds, D. (1995) 'Using school effectiveness knowledge for children with special needs — The problems and possibilities'. In C. Clark, A. Dyson and A. Millward (Eds.) *Towards Effective Schools?* London: David Fulton.

Schon, D. A. (1983) *The Reflective Practitioner: How Professionals Think in Action*. London: Temple Smith.

Stradling, R., Saunders, L. and Weston, P. (1991) *Differentiation in Action*. Slough: NFER for DES.

Thacker, J. (1982) *Steps to Success*. Windsor: NFER — NELSON.

Thompson, D. and Barton, L. (1992) 'The wider context: A free market'. *British Journal of Special Education*, 19, 1, pp. 13–15.

Wiltshire LEA (1992) *Differentiating the Secondary Curriculum*. Trowbridge: Wiltshire LEA.

Wolfendale, S. (1989) *Parental Involvement: Developing Networks Between Schools, Home and Community*. London: Cassell.

Printed in the United Kingdom for HMSO
Dd301897 3/96 C3 G3397 10170